Praise for *Agile Kata*

W0050281

"Some of the great inventions come from putting seemingly disparate things together. Joe brought together scientific thinking, practiced through Kata, with Agile philosophies and methods and came up with something more powerful than either alone. Read this book and bring Agile to life!"

—Jeffrey Liker, author of *Toyota Way*

"*Agile Kata* draws on Joe Krebs's decades of experience increasing companies' ability to respond to continuous changes in the world and in the market. It's a literal survival guide for companies navigating the uncertainty of a twenty-first century business environment."

—Jeff Gothelf, coauthor of *Who Does What by How Much?*,
Sense & Respond, and *Lean UX*

"Joe Krebs combines Agile methods with the scientific approach of Kata for continuous improvement in *Agile Kata*. As someone who has applied Toyota Kata in product management, I've seen firsthand how these practices help teams reflect, adjust, and become more effective—just as Agile principles encourage. This book offers practical guidance to help Agile teams do the same, making it an essential read for anyone looking to enhance their Agile practices."

—Melissa Perri, CEO of Product Institute and author of *Escaping the Build Trap*

"The secret to success for business leaders is not in the application of tools but rather the thinking and human capability behind them. In *Agile Kata*, Joe Krebs has created an accessible, practical, and enjoyable leadership book that brings together the disciplines of scientific thinking, grounded in the routines ('kata') of problem-solving and coaching for improvement. *Agile Kata* provides the learning structure for any leader or Agile practitioner seeking to create sustainable impact through innovation and continuous improvement."

—Katie Anderson, author of *Learning to Lead, Leading to Learn*

"If you're like me, you're a fan of Agile but also a fan of science; you're a fan of patterns but also a fan of experiments; you're a fan of learning but also a fan of joy. If so, you're going to love *Agile Kata*."

—Linda Rising, coauthor of *Fearless Change* and *More Fearless Change*

"Agile practices led us to new ways of working. *Agile Kata* will lead us to new ways of THINKING about new ways of working. In this book, author Joe Krebs takes us down time-honored paths to lead us to a new and joyful destination in our work lives."

—Richard Sheridan, author of *Joy, Inc.: How We Built a Workplace People Love*

"With this book, Joe provides a fresh perspective on Agile. As continuous learning is at the heart of agility, Agile Kata are a great means to make this a practice. The great analogies and Joe's vast experience make this book particularly compelling."

—Jutta Eckstein, coauthor of *Company-wide Agility with BOSSA nova*

"I've been observing the Agile world moving from frameworks to more holistic patterns lately. To quote Joe, 'Kata are thinking models, not operating models... Kata are closer to a pattern that is applied, and something new and exciting emerges as a result of it.' Joe's book is an incredibly important step in our Agile journey toward patterns-based approaches. I applaud him for writing it and encourage you to dive deeply into *Agile Kata*."

—Bob Galen, author and coach at Agile Moose

"Reading this book is a learning experience that enables you to nurture a learning culture for your own organization. The concepts and practical guidelines here explain how to use small experiments to build a foundation for continuous improvement. The Agile Kata approach fits any 'flavor' of modern software development."

—Lisa Crispin, consultant and coauthor of *Agile Testing* and *More Agile Testing*

"As an Agilist, I loved the original *Toyota Kata* books but struggled to grasp how to apply their powerful concepts outside manufacturing. This book—especially Joe's use cases—makes it easy to see how to use kata effectively in an Agile context."

—Fortune Buchholz, enterprise coach

AGILE KATA

PATTERNS AND PRACTICES FOR TRANSFORMATIVE ORGANIZATIONAL AGILITY

JOE KREBS

✦ Addison-Wesley

Hoboken, New Jersey

Library of Congress Control Number: 2024947089

ISBN-13: 978-0-13-811830-3
ISBN-10: 0-13-811830-2

1 2024

Melanie:

Thank you for your endless support.

Megan, Charlotte, and Alexander:

It is a wonderful, imperfect world out there. Enjoy the experiments!

In Memoriam:

Ute

Contents

Foreword by Jeff Sutherland

In the ever-evolving landscape of Agile, the need to continuously refine and elevate our practices is paramount. As someone who has spent decades shaping and refining Scrum, I am particularly excited to see the emergence of Agile Kata as a powerful pattern to bridge the gap between the structured Agile frameworks we know today and the dynamic, continuous improvement mindset that is so vital to sustained success.

My journey with Scrum began more than 30 years ago with the simple yet profound idea that small, cross-functional teams could achieve remarkable productivity by focusing on empirical process control and iterative improvement. This idea has grown into a global movement, transforming industries and revolutionizing the way we think about work. Yet, even as Scrum has matured, there has always been a need for methods that drive the mindset of continuous improvement—a mindset that is at the heart of what we aim to achieve with the Agile Kata.

The "First Principles in Scrum," which I introduced, underline this necessity. By focusing on principles like "Teams That Finish Early Accelerate Faster," we emphasize the importance of minimizing waste, optimizing flow, and enabling teams to learn and adapt faster than their competitors. The Agile Kata complements these principles by providing a structured approach to embedding continuous improvement into the daily lives of Agile teams, allowing them to tackle challenges with a scientific mindset and a relentless focus on learning.

The importance of this book cannot be overstated. It provides a much-needed pattern for integrating the kata mindset into Agile practices, offering practical insights and real-world examples that demonstrate how this integration can drive both individual and organizational excellence. By doing so, it not only enhances the effectiveness of Agile teams but also ensures that they remain adaptable, resilient, and focused on delivering maximum value in an increasingly complex world.

I had the privilege of witnessing the transformative power of continuous improvement firsthand at PatientKeeper, where we adopted early forms of these practices that contributed to a remarkable increase in both employee engagement and organizational performance. These experiences reinforced my belief that the Agile Kata is not just another tool—it is a critical mindset shift that every Agile practitioner should embrace.

As you embark on this journey with Joe Krebs's *Agile Kata*, I encourage you to approach it with the same curiosity and openness to learning that has fueled the Agile movement from the beginning. This book will challenge you, inspire you, and, most importantly, equip you with the tools and mindset needed to navigate the complexities of modern work with agility and grace.

—Jeff Sutherland
cocreator of Scrum and Scrum@Scale
Massachusetts, 2024

Foreword by Nigel Thurlow

Many organizations have struggled trying to implement a copy/paste approach to "becoming Agile," which has yielded less-than-satisfactory results. The desire to rapidly implement case-based approaches, where you study one organization's success and copy what they did, assuming it will work the same way for you, has proven false. This is the domain of big consulting houses—"It worked there so it'll work here," typically visualized in glossy PowerPoint decks. Context matters.

As my dear departed friend Ritsuo Shingo said to me many years ago, "You have to find your own way." Don't copy.

Why Agile Kata? In my opinion, Agile needs a helping hand to gain a renewed impetus. Kata describes a repeatable system of individual training exercises for practitioners of martial arts. *Toyota Kata* from Mike Rother took that same concept to help practitioners develop problem-solving and continuous improvement and muscle memory. In *Agile Kata*, Joe has taken this a step further by focusing on Agile and combining the practice of two types of Kata defined by Mike Rother.

Most organizations adopt a methodology, conduct training, hire some PDF-wielding "experts," and sit back to experience suboptimal results. Many "transformations" lack the discipline required to be successful, and most lack leadership engagement and participation at all levels. With Agile Kata, Joe aims to address both of these problems.

Joe isn't reinventing Agile; instead, he's giving you a powerful approach that teaches you a scientific thinking approach as described by Mike Rother. Yet don't be fooled into thinking discipline is not needed; it is! However, Joe breaks this down into simple steps to strengthen your application of the ideas from Agile and iterative software development and provides you with an additional scaffold to aid learning and adoption.

Joe has included some common Agile patterns in this book to bring you Agile Kata. A way to support your adoption and, if you are failing, a way to rescue that adoption. No silver bullets, just commonsense scientific thinking, discipline, and some repeatable routines that will help you and your teams develop simple habits. The result should be a better Agile process, greater agility as innovation is allowed to emerge, and happier team members as they are given the support they so often lack when adopting a change in their way of working.

If you're involved in complex work, Joe helps you understand ways to know "where you are now" by highlighting the Cynefin framework in a simple and easy-to-understand way—important when defining your current condition. He then guides you on how to move forward knowing what type of environment you are dealing with—essential when setting a target condition. If these are new terms for you then you are in for a treat. Dig in now!

If you are a change management professional, there is much to take away from this book. No one likes forced change. *Agile Kata* provides change agents a way to make change more natural, involving those impacted by the change and enabling them to learn new habits without a forced adoption.

I think you will enjoy this book. I enjoyed reviewing it.

—Nigel Thurlow
cocreator of The Flow System
Texas, 2024

Preface

If you're reading this book, you probably have some familiarity with Agile methods, maybe even a high level of expertise. But perhaps you have less knowledge of kata and have not thought a great deal about how kata and Agile can work together. That is what this book is about.

I am a long-term practitioner and deeply rooted in Agile. I've been helping clients solve their business challenges by adopting Agile processes for more than two decades. I could have stuck with Agile and helped it evolve and perhaps been perfectly content. But I came across a book that got me thinking critically about what I had learned and done with Agile. That book is called *Toyota Kata*[1] by Mike Rother, a title you can find on the bookshelf of many Lean folk. Mike is a Lean thought leader and the coauthor of *Learning to See*,[2] which is a technical book about creating continuous flow and value stream mapping. As I have also experienced in the Agile world, Mike was disappointed with the sustainability of the methods. Build a beautiful, high-functioning house of cards and then watch it collapse. He wanted something more. His conclusion was that what Toyota had that made it work, and what many companies lack, is scientific thinking.

When you approach Agile as a toolkit, you end up with nice-looking artifacts that may have little to do with how the work actually gets done, similar to the way an outdated map doesn't match the scenery you see in front of you. In fact, everyone faces problems in their daily work, and the idea of continuous improvement is to recognize them, try to understand why they occur, and solve them rather than let them fester indefinitely. Along come Lean and Agile, and now you have new tools to throw at the problems. However, the tools themselves do not solve the problems or help you reach your goals. The tools can be helpful if you think a certain way. Mike called that certain way "scientific thinking."

This way of thinking is not much different from the general concept of science. Confront the facts or the actual situation honestly, set clear goals, and experiment your way to the goals by trying out your ideas. This is different from either throwing general tools at the problem or assuming that your general theory about what should work in this situation is true. Humans have all sorts of cognitive biases, and we often assume we know things that we do not. We also are pretty bad at accepting that the world is a complex place filled with uncertainty. We know much less than we do not know.

So Mike Rother came up with a general model of scientific thinking that he called *Improvement Kata*. But the point was not to develop yet another problem-solving model. The point was to develop a general pattern of scientific thinking and then teach it by doing. You don't implement

---

1. [MR2009]

2. [MRJS1999]

kata, but you practice it. The term *kata* comes from the martial arts—breaking down complex physical skills into small pieces and then practicing them one by one to master each skill. Put them together, and you can begin to learn how to defend yourself.

Mike Rother's book includes many references to manufacturing and physical objects in the production process. And the book *Toyota Kata* does not mention the word *agile* even once throughout the entire book. Don't let that scare you off. Mike developed these concepts after observing scientific thinking at Toyota, and most of his practice was in manufacturing at first. It may be easier to practice on repetitive, manual processes, but it applies equally well to knowledge work and for teams building products in Agile teams.

Once I saw that kata is a meta-skill and can be of universal use, it quickly became my friend for Agile transformations. In more recent years, I learned through my work and from feedback from other Agile Kata practitioners that the pattern can be applied in many ways to increase agility. It represents *Patterns and Practices for Transformative Organizational Agility*, which is the subtitle of this book.

As you work your way through this book, you will notice two different uses of Improvement Kata. The first is a way of thinking through repeated practice. The goal is to rewire your brain so that you naturally think scientifically when approaching any of life's goals. That does not mean that you pull out the kata and try to follow it exactly, but it becomes a natural way of thinking applied in different ways to different situations.

A second use is to consider the pattern of Improvement Kata as a good model for working toward your goals, like software that helps users achieve their goals with minimum fuss and frustration. This is using the kata like an Agile process that you can integrate with existing Agile methods and thinking or replace the one you're currently using. I often use it this way.

I will go back and forth in usage. Please excuse me for that. I love the idea of practicing scientific thinking, and I love the Agile Kata pattern as a way to strengthen Agile organizations. Mike Rother and his colleague Jeff Liker remind everyone in their publications *Toyota Kata* and *The Toyota Way* that Kata is mainly a way to practice and develop scientific thinking. I will keep using kata in both ways and keep learning and experimenting with other ways so we can increase agility.

Acknowledgments

Thanks

I want to thank all the wonderful colleagues and friends who were part of my learning journey and career. That journey included stops at Mercedes Benz Group AG, ParcPlace Digitalk, Valtech, IBM, and AOL.

A big shout out to all the coaches and trainers who have contributed to the success of my company Incrementor for more than 15 years.

Thank you to my clients for trusting me as an advisor and utilizing my coaching and training services.

Thank you all for being part of my journey that somehow culminated in *Agile Kata*.

Special Mentions

Mike Rother, thank you for your research and for publishing *Toyota Kata*, the starting point of my kata journey. Thank you also for welcoming me with open arms to the kata community and for giving me the opportunity to meet so many like-minded kata professionals.

Dr. Jeffrey Liker, thank you for being such an important voice in the review and writing process. Thank you for taking so much time to go through chapters, refine, and collaborate on the intersection of Agile and kata. It was a truly unique experience.

Nigel Thurlow, first and foremost, thank you for providing a foreword and seeing the vision of this book. Your practical experiences with the Toyota Production System and Agile processes made this an invaluable and insightful review process with you.

Feedback

Thank you Alexander Alarid, Fortune Buchholz, Lisa Crispin, Luke Hohmann, Dave Horecny, Rolf Irion, Ralph Jocham, Joanna Plaskonka, Karl Scotland, Richard Sheridan, Rikard Skelander, Jim Sparks, and John R. Turner for offering invaluable feedback at various stages in the writing process. The finished book would not be the same without your contributions.

Cover and Illustrations

Jim Nuttle created the book cover and illustrations. I have collaborated with Jim for several previous projects, including live visual recordings at conferences, educational posters, and even fun stickers. His work is stellar, and I have a feeling that you will enjoy his work, too. Thank you, Jim.

Publishing and Editorial Team

Thank you Haze Humbert for being transparent and supportive throughout the entire process. You have been a great sounding board and help from the initial book idea to the final product that was delivered to the readers.

I also want to thank the entire Pearson team that has helped with the production of this title, in particular Menka Mehta, Julie Nahil, Charlotte Kughen, Tricia Bronkella, Karen Davis, and Johnna VanHoose Dinse. Their attention to detail in the editing process and final stages of production was incredible. Thank you all.

About the Author

Joe (Jochen) Krebs (www.joekrebs.com) is a German-American computer scientist, consultant, and entrepreneur. As the founder of Incrementor, an Agile consultancy, Joe has collaborated with hundreds of companies across various industries, driving significant improvements in their Agile practices. His global client list includes start-ups and Fortune 500 companies alike. Joe is a community builder, podcast host, speaker, and author. He lives in Westchester, near New York City.

In conjunction with *Agile Kata*, Joe has established Agile Kata Pro (www.agilekata.pro), where you can find valuable resources, courses, and tools for your professional Agile Kata journey.

Introduction

Agile Kata is new. Both topics individually, Agile and kata, are not. They have long histories on their own. They have proven themselves time and again and their communities are strong. Both believe in similar things. My hope is to connect them, and perhaps many other Agile professionals will have an aha moment similar to what I experienced when I began moving the puzzle pieces closer together.

In recent years, I have seen a burst of new fresh ideas flooding the Agile community. At the time of writing this book, I noticed a positive trend and energy toward organizational design, enterprise and team coaching, business agility, agile leadership, scaling, and portfolio management. There was also an appetite to learn ways to improve the process of an Agile team. The beautiful thing is that Agile Kata can help you get started with all of these topics. And if you've already started with one of them, Agile Kata can help you continuously improve it.

Agile Kata is *a* universal pattern, not *the* universal pattern. I can't predict the future. No one can. But from what I can tell about recent trends, businesses have adapted to leaner and flatter hierarchies. Some companies have established democratic, self-managed workplaces with great success. Employees entering the job market are looking for purpose, learning, and growth as a person—and, of course, reward. A fail fast and learn attitude, courage for experimentation, and closing feedback loops with stakeholders and customers is becoming the new norm everywhere. All of these trends are deeply anchored in Agile and scientific thinking and are directly linked to Agile Kata, which can enable these.

Purpose, Background, and Goals

Back in the mid-1990s, when I developed software in Smalltalk, I had the chance to experiment with a series of processes that were fundamentally different from what was commonly used. I used the Rational Unified Process (RUP), Ivar Jacobson's use-case-driven approach, and Extreme Programming (XP). Compared to today, this pre-Agile-Manifesto period before 2001 truly felt like a groundbreaking, revolutionary era. Some might have referred to us as a bunch of corporate rebels. Even though I was at the beginning of my career, I already had firsthand experience with the flaws of waterfall. I felt anxious to try something new, but we didn't have the data and evidence yet to be sure that new ways of working would revolutionize the future. In hindsight, this was a bold move to branch off into a niche, especially because I was so early in my career.

The Agile Manifesto did a wonderful job bringing the various processes and frameworks together under one umbrella by giving it a name, values, and a set of principles. I vividly remember taking a trip to Newton, Massachusetts, shortly after the Agile Manifesto was released because news made it to me in New York City that "a guy" named Jeff Sutherland would give a training on Scrum. I felt that I had to be part of that session, especially after I read *Agile Software Development with Scrum (Pearson)*,[1] which was fresh off the press. So I made my way up toward Boston…

The training took place in an improvised back room at PatientKeeper, where Jeff worked at that time. It was a small class, and I felt like an intruder because a regular workday unfolded next to us while we were learning about Scrum. Because of the circumstances where Scrum was being taught, it felt like a well-kept secret. That is what moonshiners during prohibition must have felt like.

When I reflect on the past, I recognize that moments like that were important stepping stones in my career. My background in various Agile processes eventually led to creating my own consultancy: Incrementor in New York. Just a few years after that trip to Boston, I had the chance to deliver scrum trainings alongside Jeff and Ken.

A similar eye-opening moment happened in the late 2010s, when the early indicators for successful Agile transformations were dismal. By looking closer at the struggles and failures of Agile transformations, it was quite noticeable that the Agile mindset we used with teams got lost when applied to the transformation process. Questions from clients, such as, "What is the process of introducing Scrum to my organization?" did not generate good answers. It felt ironic that organizations fell back into waterfall behavior when introducing Agile as their new DNA in the organization. I noticed "waves" of work and heard words like *roll-out* and *complete* used in the context of Agile transformations. These transformations were often treated as projects or as single-improvement initiatives, like an item on a corporate checklist.

The grassroots movement of Agile in the early days—where teams worked, learned, and continuously refined their process over time—seemed to have ended. Agile transformations now showed signs of top-down, command-and-control leadership. Some companies even tried to standardize their organization and aimed for _____ (fill in the Agile process flavor of your choice) conformity. Those organizations had entirely missed the idea of what Agile was all about.

In 2017, when I began reading *Toyota Kata* (McGraw Hill) by Mike Rother, I had this instant feeling that scientific thinking trained by kata and continuous improvement could be of tremendous value for the Agile community. Even though Rother uses Toyota as a vehicle (no pun intended) to bring that pattern to surface, it's really not about Toyota and cars at all. Once I saw that the kata is a meta skill and can be of universal use, it became my friend for Agile transformations and so much more. Let's explore this further.

During the hype of Agile transformations, I noticed an abundance of promises made by companies selling shiny Agile transformation playbooks. Those start-to-finish processes were often just a fancy name for an old-school waterfall process that made the planned transformation look logical, safe, and easy to buy in. Many learned the hard way that this is far from reality. I know of several large companies that had several unsuccessful transformations, until they decided to

---

1. [KSMB2001]

give up. Maybe it is time to question the playbooks and the approaches instead of questioning the ability of an organization to change. I would even argue that every company can change. The question instead is: How fast can they change?

The difference between the traditional approach and kata is also captured in the well-known saying, "Give a man a fish, and you feed him for a day; teach a man to fish and you feed him for a lifetime." Just handing an organization a blueprint and sending a constant stimulus from the outside to become more agile is clearly not enough. On the other hand, Toyota Kata is that meta skill that teaches an organization to learn how to fish. As a matter of fact, it teaches how to fish and continuously improve your fishing skills. Learning is continuous.

But when I began increasing agility this way, I remembered the quote by Antoine de Saint-Exupéry: "If you want to build a ship, don't drum up people to collect wood and don't assign them tasks and work, but rather teach them to long for the endless immensity of the sea."

Agility is the resiliency in an organization to make better, more rapid decisions in response to feedback with the purpose of building better products and services. To stay relevant as a for-profit company, reading the market trends and reacting accordingly is extremely important. The successful companies are really good at this.

Agile Kata extends Toyota Kata in ways to embrace and live by Agile values and principles from day one. Enabling an Agile culture by adopting a new leadership style increases collaborating skills in self-organized, autonomous teams. It also requires an upgrade of coaching skills and ways of measuring the success of our products and the process.

In the beginning, my goals were very narrow. I wanted to help clients in their transformation journey. We tested kata ideas and experimented in various settings. The feedback was positive, and we got encouragement to continue. We created the Agile Transformation Kata as the first attempt to formalize the pattern and name it. Then we dropped the word *transformation* after we learned about many additional scenarios that went way beyond the initial transformation need.

I hope this book will give you plenty of new ideas to help increase agility. The ideas in it will challenge the ways things currently work in your organization and help you consider how using Agile Kata can make it a better place. Considering that agile organizations are more flexible and adaptable and therefore more competitive, I believe that Agile Kata can be of tremendous value for your company or client. Another hope, which might sound very ambitious and audacious, is that Agile Kata can help your organization and the Agile community as a whole to break through stalemate situations to reach a higher level of agility.

The goal of the book is neither a full introduction to kata nor to Agile nor a resource to make you an expert on either topic. It would be a false expectation to think something so big could be covered in only a couple hundred pages or to expect that you can develop skills only by reading. However, this book should get you off the ground.

If I have left out a reference to your favorite Lean, Agile, or kata book, it doesn't mean that it's not relevant in the context of Agile Kata. It's tough for an author to find a balance between the right amount of relevant information and paralyzing the reader through information overload. Again, I hope I have kept the content focused so that you can navigate the topic effectively.

This book is relatively short by design. It may take you only a few days to read through the material. The Agile Kata approach is very lightweight, just like other Agile processes, and the length of this book carries that spirit. However, keep in mind that lightweight does not necessarily mean that it is also easy to do.

You will certainly encounter challenges when you apply Agile Kata within your environment. Over time, though, if you practice it deliberately, it will become second nature.

My goal with this book is to build a solid bridge between kata and Agile—a bridge that should make you feel comfortable to cross in either direction. To do this, I chose a mix of theory, examples, and use cases that should give you plenty of confidence to introduce Agile Kata to your organization. I'm curious to hear about your success stories, but if you notice that it is not working the way you expect, please let me know, too. To keep this process interactive, I have reserved www.joekrebs.com/agile-kata-book, where you can submit any feedback about the content of the book. For training-, certification-, and community-related inquiries, please visit www.agilekata.pro, a hub created for Agile Kata professionals. For book content and feedback, please visit joekrebs.com/agile-kata-book.

Who Should Read this Book?

The kata by itself is a universal pattern for any kind of improvement, and Part I could be especially beneficial for *anyone* who wants to improve any situation, Agile or not.

Parts II and III connect the kata with Agile ways of working. For example, if you are in the role of an Agile coach, scrum master, project manager, or change agent whose goal is to increase agility, all three parts of this book should give you fresh new ideas and tools to improve. Because Agile Kata is a universal pattern that touches potentially any type of team, testers, developers, architects, and user-interface designers can get some fresh new ideas for working together as well—in that case, as an IT team.

If you are an executive or leader, Agile Kata can give you new ideas for implementing Agile strategies, effecting cultural change, and transforming organizational design. You may also consider using Agile Kata to provide a new way of working with your peers or teams.

If you are a member of a project management office or portfolio management team, Agile Kata can spark new ideas and create additional viewpoints using experimentation, goals, or targets.

Change agents looking for a new change-management process that introduces more agility to their organization will hopefully find new inspiration in Agile Kata.

Last but not least, members of a product management team may use Agile Kata for designing new ways to interact with their stakeholders and build product visions and product strategies. They may even use Agile Kata for building the actual product. Agile Kata is as universal as it is exciting.

Whatever your motivations are when you decided to read about this topic, I hope you find it refreshingly new and that you gain a new perspective. If you find more success as a result of using the kata, I would be thrilled to know. Beware: Applying Agile Kata is highly addictive and may captivate you beyond reading this book. (At least that is what happened to me when I started my journey.)

How This Book Is Organized

I can't wait to show you what kata are all about and how kata and Agile complement each other. Even more importantly, I want to show you what you can do with the kata day by day. You will notice how these three goals of the book map directly to the table of contents.

Part I provides you with a foundation and introduction to kata and scientific thinking and explains what makes kata in general so unique. You will see that a mindset of scientific thinking can be very different compared to well-established Agile processes and frameworks. If you are contemplating using kata outside the boundaries of Agile, Part I is your companion. If you're already familiar with kata, you may skim through this part of the book, although I think I offer a perspective that appeals to Agile practitioners and may be new to you. The main goal of Part I is to set the stage for Part II and eventually Part III.

After the foundation of the kata is laid in Part I, we explore how Agile ways of working can extend the basic form of the kata. Part II takes important Agile topics and links those to the kata: coaching, culture, collaboration, measuring value, and leadership, to name a few and give you food for thought and context. You can see each topic as an extension point to the original basic kata form that's covered in Part I. At the end of Part II, you will have a better understanding of Agile Kata.

While you are reading through the first two parts of the book, you will probably generate tons of wonderful ideas for improving agility in your team or organization as a whole. In my experience since I began working with Agile Kata, the sky is truly the limit. You can go as far as your creativity and practice will take you.

After reading Part II, you might feel ready and impatient to get started. But before you do that, check out Part III, where I share a set of common use cases. These use cases may validate some of the ideas you generate while reading through Parts I and II. By sharing these vastly different but common use cases for Agile practitioners, I hope I inspire you to identify Agile Kata opportunities. I'm confident that at least one of the use cases will stand out as your personal starting point with Agile Kata. But I wouldn't be surprised if you find more than one use case that connects well with what you would like to improve within your team or organization. In this case you will face the difficult choice of which to start with—which is not a bad problem to have.

I used the word *common* rather than *typical* to describe the use cases in Part III. Although the words seem to be interchangeable, there are minor differences. In the complex and exciting world that we live in, the word *common* implies something that is generally encountered in various situations. *Typical,* on the other hand, refers to something that is expected to happen; it's more of a standard. The difference is nuanced, but it's important when you work through the scenarios during Part III. When navigating the unknown with scientific thinking and Agile Kata, be prepared to be surprised. Instead of applying each use case as-is, like an exact recipe, the use cases should serve you only as a starting point.

The point of Agile Kata is not to provide a set of generic solutions to generic problems. Every organization or team has unique characteristics and parameters, and every client solution is unique as well. Thus, you're working to achieve the goals of your products for your users based on the experiences and knowledge of your team.

The main benefit of the use cases is to stimulate some ideas about where Agile Kata might be useful and how it can be used. Although every situation is unique, I hope you will find inspiration in Part III to start trying this new pattern.

Throughout the book, you will discover the occasional links to additional resources, such as activities or material you might find useful when applying Agile Kata. In addition, each chapter ends with a set of reflection questions to let the topic sink in a little more.

Challenges

Writer's block is defined as, "The inability to begin or continue writing for reasons other than a lack of basic skill or commitment."[2] Many writers, including myself, have encountered writer's block before, but if you use Gerry Weinberg's fieldstone method,[3] writer's block is almost a thing of the past. *Almost…*

There are still unforeseen events that can cause a book project that has lasted for almost two years to derail at any given time. In my case, it was a death in the family, a severe weather impact in Florida, and a lost passport that prevented me from traveling internationally for months. Situations like this make it hard to get back into the groove of writing again. Ironically, many Agile initiatives that get stuck somewhere in their journey have similarities to writer's block for an author. A new fieldstone, or kata, unblocked me and kept me going.

Positive events can also have an impact on the writing process. During a project like this, the life of a consultant continues, and clients were asking for Agile Kata training and coaching services.

2. [MR2009]

3. [GW2005]

Conference organizers began inquiring about Agile Kata presentations, which I gladly accepted to keep spreading the word. The appetite for Agile Kata also continued in the form of webinars, user group events, and podcasts. These events made it easy to transition back to writing and helped me to see opportunities for Agile Kata from even more angles.

PART I

KATA

What is *kata*? If you studied the martial arts, you probably already know and have experienced kata. If you watched the *Karate Kid* or the follow-up *Cobra Kai*, you also should know. Martial arts is very complex and involves your body doing things it was not meant to do. Simply watching a black belt at work is interesting, but it's useless for learning the skills.

Fortunately, the apparent complexity of skills has been broken into pieces to make learning easier. There's a right way to do each micro skill, and each is a kata. It is something to practice, with a coach giving you feedback. As you master more kata, you have more tools in the toolbox for a fight. With practice, each skill becomes natural, like muscle memory, and you can focus on the fight rather than the individual skills. Those of you who have learned to play a musical instrument, cook, dance, or paint with the help of a good teacher have learned through kata even though it was not called that.

Scientific thinking helps us change existing habits that are hard to overcome. One way to change how we think is to practice a new way of thinking, one kata at a time. We have a four-step model and developed routines to practice scientific thinking.

Part I of this book introduces the basic concepts of Improvement Kata and Coaching Kata. (That's right, we also have a kata for the coach to practice.) In Part II, I connect kata to the practices of Agile.

I've already used *kata*, which I understand might be a brand new term for you, heavily. It is my goal in this part to break it down into digestible pieces.

Kata Mindset

If you read the Preface and Introduction, you already got a glimpse into the background of kata. Are you ready to explore what the kata mindset is and how you can use it to jump-start scientific thinking?

Scientific thinking enables us to deal with uncertainty, complexity, cultural challenges, and changing habits. I cover all those topics in this chapter. Before I get to that, I want to define kata and take a closer look at its origins.

Kata Definition

The word *kata* can take different interpretations when translated from Japanese to English. One of them is form or way of doing—for example, in the way of doing Agile or the way of transforming to Agile. A different interpretation is a pattern of movements that is deliberately practiced. Learning new skills and combining them with deliberate practice has been a very common and successful approach for many centuries across many disciplines—for example in the world of education, cooking, music, and sports.

In the business world, we often learn very differently. Instead of experimenting and learning by doing, new ways of working are often shared more passively. For example, have you ever heard colleagues meet with the goal to "align" but then later realize that they still are not aligned? Real and deep cultural change can't be effective when new ways of working are shared only via email. Products today also are not created based on one single idea. Culture, products, and processes evolve organically, and incorporating experimentation can be a powerful tool for change.

During my career, I've had quite a few surprises with change management. First, I was surprised by the amount of time and effort that went into the planning stages of the change management process only to learn that the results ranged from unorganized to even chaotic. Lengthy planning activities didn't pay off. Shooting from the hip and applying gut-feeling decision-making are common signs of the opposite behavior. Luck might make decision-makers successful on occasion, but that is not a good strategy, in my opinion.

A kata mindset, on the other hand, introduces a pattern for learning and practicing new skills in a business world, very similar to what people are used to in sports. That's why the word *kata*, which has its roots in martial arts, works so well.

Other authors refer to kata as a routine, practice, process, or even a model. All good options, but I prefer *pattern* over the other terms because patterns are solutions to recurring problems.[1] How to improve or change an organization can be a recurring and continuous problem. Kata are universal in their application and have been proven for many years to solve common challenges. Patterns give you confidence because they have been successfully applied in similar situations before.

In case you're wondering, the plural of *kata* is still *kata*, not *katas*.

Habits

We all have habits that are part of our day-to-day activities. You might also call them routines. For example, a morning routine might involve how you make coffee or the sequence of activities to get ready for a workday. But habits were not always habits. They became habits over time as you practiced them over and over again. They became habits through repetition.

Every time you repeat a certain behavior, the neurological pathways in your brain become stronger. Because they become stronger, they become your default mode over time. Your brain likes this default mode because it is much easier to make decisions, and you don't have to expend as much energy.

The human brain weighs 2 percent compared to our overall body weight, but it uses 20 percent of the overall energy.[2] As the human body is looking for areas to conserve energy, which is part

---

1.   [GHJV1995]

2.   https://www.ncbi.nlm.nih.gov/pmc/articles/PMC8364152/

of our survival mode, the brain stands out as an ideal candidate to save energy. The phrase "Don't even think about it!" is a subtle reminder that thinking is an effort. Routines help conserve energy.

Look at routines in your life. For example, do you take the same route to work every morning, even though there are possibly many alternatives? When you encounter a random detour, do you feel out of your element and need to think harder to adjust to the new situation?

In decision-making, the habit-driven default mode is very powerful because our brains are already trained for a specific action. The brain pathways for default mode are strong and ready to go. Not only does the default mode conserve energy, but it is quick, and the steps associated with a specific action are easy to execute. They became second nature because of repetition.

Another reason why default mode works so well is rooted in evolution. When humans face a dangerous situation, we run and hide. A mass panic is unfortunately proof that many people react very similarly when facing the same critical situation. Going into analysis mode in the face of danger or stopping to prepare a plan of action is not a good idea for obvious reasons. Waiting and seeing could be even worse. Habits make us behave quickly in a certain, practiced way, which is important when we face a decision where time is of the essence. Otherwise the human race wouldn't be what it is today. It is literally a no-brainer.

Repetition and Habits

However, default mode is not always our friend. For example, picture yourself in the driver's seat of a parked car. You are about to open the door and exit the car. How would you do it? People in the Netherlands learn to open the door with the hand farthest away from the door. It is called the "Dutch Reach."[3] Opening the door with the far hand forces the person to turn their shoulders, making it easier to turn the neck and to explore the blind spot for other cars, cyclists, or pedestrians (Figure 1.1), which can cause an accident called "dooring." This small habitual change saves lives and many injuries—more than you might think. But in New York City alone, seven people died from being "doored" between 1996 and 2005, and many more were injured. In Chicago, 344 were doored and injured in the year 2011 alone. That is almost one person a day in only one major city. In Germany, it is estimated that every second accident between a bicyclist and parked car is related to "dooring."[4]

---

3. https://www.nytimes.com/2018/10/05/smarter-living/the-dutch-reach-save-bicyclists-lives-bicycle-safety-drivers.html

4. dutchreach.org

Figure 1.1
Dutch Reach

Using the Dutch Reach when you open the car door seems like an easy fix to this problem, doesn't it? So why don't we all do it? Well, changing the way we open a car door is actually not as easy as you might think. We're back to these neural pathways that have been trained through frequent repetition. In this case, people have practiced and reinforced a suboptimal behavior, and because opening a car door is such a frequent activity, often performed many times a day, our neural pathways are especially strong, like neurological super highways.

If you are familiar with bicycle traffic in Amsterdam, you probably have an idea why the Dutch Reach originated in the Netherlands. Interestingly enough, the technique has no name among the Dutch; it's just the way they open car doors because they learned it that way. They learn it in driving school and, most importantly, they practice it. Deliberate practice turns it into a habit. Simply placing a flyer explaining the Dutch Reach into the glove compartment of every newly sold car wouldn't have the same effect as learning it in driving school and practicing it repeatedly. Similarly, when practiced deliberately, kata are patterns that will form and establish new habits.

Experimentation

Another concern about habits is the lack of context to make informed decisions. These organizational blind spots are dangerous because our default mode of conserving energy and making decisions quickly (survival mode) can easily send us back to old behavior. Blind spots are everywhere in our lives, not only in the literal sense of opening a car door. A kata can change our behavior by helping us recognize blind spots and deal with them in a more scientific manner.

We learn deeper in the process of doing, not before. As a matter of fact, learning and forecasting capabilities increase drastically once we start practicing something. Agile teams often experience this phenomena when team members begin working on a certain task. A team might start working on an item and then decide it wants to re-estimate it because the item changed significantly as the team worked. The team then compares its experience gained by doing work with the experience it had prior to starting the work.

Once you are working on a task, you're most likely learning something about the activity that you didn't know when you started. That's kind of obvious, isn't it? Everyone knows from life experience that things often don't work out the way they were planned. I'm sure you have plenty of examples in your personal and professional lives. But then why are we building grand start-to-end plans for products, teams, transformations, or culture change? Do these plans exist to give us a false sense of certainty and predictably? Or are these just habits that we have learned through traditional project management in the past? Kata doesn't mean that you skip the planning, but you will see that it is done in a very different way.

Kata practitioners apply scientific thinking. That means we trust facts because facts are friendly. Taiichi Ohno reminds us that "Data is of course important in manufacturing, but I place the greatest emphasis on facts."[5] Facts are supported by data—quantitative or qualitative. Using facts and a delta between the current and desired state, kata practitioners use experiments to close the gap. As soon as they close the gap, they define another desired (next) state and so forth.

Experimenting is something taught in school, but surprisingly, people seem to have lost that skill in the business world. Maybe it is because experiments can fail, and some leaders may have a negative association with failed experiments. Do failed experiments imply failure in job performance? Certainly not. It is that mindset shift that requires certain cultural change.

The kata mindset brings that exploratory and experimental mindset back into organizations one step at a time. This does not mean that we are all becoming scientists but that we're using scientific thinking. Let's take a closer look at what that could be like at the highest possible level.

To get started, you need a challenge or goal. Ultimately, it is a goal that provides context and turns a group of people into a team. The difference between a group of people and a team is that a team is interdependent, has a shared goal, and has the skills necessary to reach that goal. One of the skills could be to acquire new skills—a meta skill, if you want to see it that way. Kata is exactly that meta skill.

For example, picture an elevator filled with strangers. What are they typically doing? You often see people checking their phones, looking at the floor or ceiling, or staring at elevator buttons. Typically, there is hardly any conversation or communication among the occupants. It is not needed because everyone has a personal goal of reaching their destination as quickly as possible. But what happens if the elevator gets stuck?

---

5.   [TO1988]

Once we have a goal or challenge (Step 1), we need an understanding of our current situation (Step 2). Having evidence about the current situation is an important step in a scientific mindset. It is important to not jump to conclusions when trying to solve a problem. Without having a good understanding of the current situation, you will most likely solve the wrong problem or apply a suboptimal solution. For this reason, I remind everyone new to Agile Kata about my mantra: "Don't kata corners!"

The goal could be very big, and the step from the current situation to that goal way too long. Your aim is to define a small step (Step 3) that gets you closer to the goal. Having a goal and the awareness of where you currently are enables you to define a small next step. The delta between "is" and "next" has now opened up a playing field for experimentation (Step 4). One or more experiments need to be conducted to reach that desired next target. To point out the difference to other Agile processes, you aren't planning the path between the current condition and the next target condition. You're planning the experiments you believe have a chance to get you there. Do one experiment at a time to stay focused and keep the results and variables isolated.

The experiments of pressing all the elevator buttons or having all people in the elevator car jump at the same time, like the scene in the movie *You've Got Mail*,[6] are examples of unsuccessful experiments to get the elevator moving again.

I get into the specifics of scientific thinking in Chapter 2. For now, I'll tell you the four basic questions that frame the overall kata approach:

1.   What is your goal or challenge?

2.   Where are you right now?

3.   What could be a small step toward the goal or challenge?

4.   Which experiment(s) could get you to the next step?

But before you go deeper into the kata itself, let's explore the kata mindset a little more.

Uncertainty

I need to emphasize again that using kata does not imply that we're all becoming scientists. It means that we're applying scientific thinking to what we do. If you've created a thesis as part of your graduate or undergraduate studies in the past, you know that this type of thinking process requires great effort. It is definitely not our default mode.

Deliberately practicing kata will help you practice your scientific thinking and eventually make it a new habit among teams, departments, or entire organizations. Kata means that you're applying a scientific thinking pattern to break existing habits and to form better ones that replace or refine the old ones.

---

6.   https://www.imdb.com/title/tt0128853/?ref_=ext_shr_lnk

In the beginning of any journey, such as an Agile transformation, you face the highest level of uncertainty. Planning an entire project or product (start to finish) at that moment is not a promising idea. This is one of the many reasons why so many companies began introducing Agile processes in the first place, but ironically, they often are doing it in a non-Agile manner. But having a kata mindset doesn't mean eliminating planning altogether.

With Agile Kata, you plan quite frequently but in much shorter segments. You wear a planning hat when you define the direction or goal. You're in planning mode when you define the current situation. You're also planning to determine the target. Three out of four steps of scientific thinking are related to planning activities. Even experiments, which can be seen as execution and doing, require a level of planning. This might sound like too much planning, but the three planning steps combined are very short in comparison to the overall time typically spent during experimentation. The time spent executing the experiments should significantly outweigh the time spent in planning. That is important because you learn from doing, not from planning.

You use the conditions to build long-term and short-term goals and to validate your results and compare them to the predictions. Because kata are continuous, planning is continuous. Kata practitioners don't rely on maps; they rely on a compass. That's why kata are so powerful when applied in situations where teams and organizations are in uncharted territory.

Cynefin,[7] developed by David Snowden,[8] is a well-known sense-making framework often used to consider the dynamics of situations, decisions, perspectives, conflicts, and changes to come to a consensus for decision-making under uncertainty. These domains provide clarification as to what type of methods, tools, or techniques may be required when operating in each. It enables executives to see things from new viewpoints, assimilate complex concepts, and address real-world problems and opportunities. Using the Cynefin framework can help executives sense which context they are in so that they can make better decisions and avoid issues that can arise when their current management style causes them to make mistakes.[9]

Kata has a sweet spot in the *complex* and *complicated* segments (Figure 1.2). *Chaotic* situations are best addressed with a clear immediate action, like a natural disaster response. The experimental approach with kata would not be a good response in that situation. The same is true for the clear segment, where the situation is stable and known and you would execute a predictable process.

To make matters even more interesting, the kata mindset assumes that the current situation is not permanent. You're not building from a solid base. The assumption is that the existing process could be fragile or wrong, so every option needs to be on the table—everything from fine-tuning an existing process all the way to replacing it.

---

7.   https://en.wikipedia.org/wiki/Cynefin_framework

8.   [DS2022]

9.   [JTNT2023]

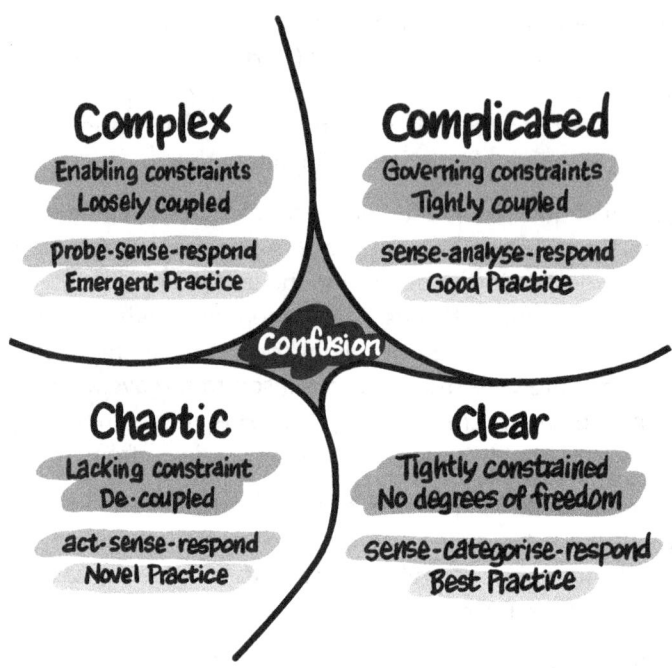

Figure 1.2
Cynefin framework (Dave Snowden, licensed under CC BY-SA 4.0.)

Cynefin is Welsh for *habitat*, and the five domains in Figure 1.2 can be seen as habitats. Kata is a pattern to change habits. Interestingly, the words *habitat* and *habit* share the same Latin root: *habitare*. Over the years, habitats become a place or environment where things live. Habits are repeated behaviors by the ones in a habitat. I'm suggesting to create a new habit (kata) to tackle situations in the complex and complicated habitats (domains). And from the other perspective, give the new habit a habitat.

Activity: Click! A One-Week Starter Routine to See the Unexpected Positively[10]

- Start each day with the counter reset to zero.

- As you go through the day, notice when something goes differently than you expected.

- Add a click each time that happens and note the unexpected for reflection later.

- At the end of the day, write down your total number of clicks for that day.

---

10.   http://tinyurl.com/clickerkata (Cascadia School World-Wide)

Continuous Improvement

Does your company launch "initiatives" to implement improvement ideas on a team or at the departmental or organizational level? Maybe you have been part of one of these initiatives—for example, a workshop to identity bottlenecks and problems followed by a project initiative to remove those bottlenecks. The result of these initiatives is often mediocre, even though the intentions are obviously very good. The problem is that it's hard to stay focused and keep the momentum of a process improvement effort for a long period. Simply eliminating waste as a strategy doesn't motivate a group of people and won't carry their interest and passion of the topic for long. A much better approach is looking at a value stream and creating a better customer experience. If you're designing that in a way that results in less waste, even better.

Introducing Agile Kata into a team or organization means focusing on solving challenges. The frequency of execution determines how continuous the improvement will be. Focusing on improvement a few weeks a year isn't enough in a rapidly changing business environment. A few improvement projects here and there aren't going to create new habits of working, just like a one-time mention of opening a car door with a different hand won't result in long-lasting behavioral change. The risk of falling back into old habits is very high if the new way of improving isn't practiced with ongoing intensity. That might be one of the reasons why so many internal improvement efforts and transformations don't stick and fall short of their promises. Underlying habit changes can't happen by having two or three improvement efforts per year. That is just not enough repetition to make the changes stick.

Changing small things every day is easier to tackle, track, and complete than large portions of improvement work spread across months or even years. Even retrospectives, possibly executed every other week, are not continuous in the sense of Agile Kata. Long-lasting, effective cultural change needs to be trained and practiced frequently. Continuous improvement, continuous adaption, and continuous innovation needs to be built into daily routines. The more you practice them, the easier they become part of your new routine. Practicing something for 15 minutes or more every day is better than practicing something for one hour a week.

As a consultant, I've met many individuals over the years who felt that real change would not be possible in their organization. Some of them were even very cynical about it. You might have a story where you have encountered attitudes like that in your organization. Like in so many companies, your story might include the idea of a status quo with process improvement in general, where teams began living with mediocre results. The answer to these attitudes might be as simple as swapping the existing change management process with an Agile Kata mindset that can transform people and organizations continuously.

Cynicism is detrimental for a company culture if it becomes entrenched within an organization. However, at the outset, cynicism shows that someone deeply cares about much needed change and is getting frustrated about it. Strong leadership can create a playing field for continuous improvement and make change transparent, day by day.

But Agile Kata is not necessarily an instant success. It will take time to get familiar with it through practice. A kata is not a tool or product that is installed or implemented. It serves as a starting point, and with more experience, you will begin evolving it closer to your specific needs. The more frequently you apply it, the better you will become at it.

In the spirit of continuous improvement, a kata mindset not only focuses on what needs to change but also on what was previously changed. Every professional soccer player practices basic drills over and over again, even though they have already done those many times during their career. Every behavior needs to be reinforced. Here's another example: I programmed in Smalltalk more than 20 years ago. Compared to someone new to Smalltalk, I would probably have an easier time working myself back into this topic again, but focusing only on what has changed in Smalltalk since I used it regularly without practicing the basics again would not bring me back to that same level. I would need to go back to the basics.

Kata are thinking models, not operating models. They are not a methodology, a framework, or solutions to be applied as-is. They serve as a starting point and should evolve—just like dancing. For example, when you learn to dance the tango, you need to memorize a specific basic step sequence. Once you learn that sequence, you can move on and incorporate more complex elements. But even at the professional dance level, a tango still looks and feels like a tango because the basic sequence is still recognizable.

Kata are practiced, although I stay away from calling them a best practice. Kata are closer to a pattern that is applied and something new and exciting emerges as a result of it. The culture of kata should be lived among the employees in an organization. They can't be only a fancy diagram hanging on a wall. Living means experiencing it firsthand. A gemba walk is an example of this, and that is where the facts are found. (Read more about gemba walks in the next section.)

Kata Culture

Elevating the kata mindset from a habit of a single person to shared habits by a group of people adds complexity because you enter the cultural level of an organization. Culture is a concept that includes social behavior, norms, rules, and capabilities shared by all individuals in a group. That behavior also includes habits. Because kata can change habits of an individual, it also can shift an entire culture of an organization.

If we can agree that it isn't easy to change a single person's behavior, as with the car door example earlier in the chapter, it's no easier to change or influence the culture of an organization. There is one company that stands out as a leader in terms of continuous improvement and adaptation, and it's where lean manufacturing originated: Toyota. Many terms you will find in this book and in other literature about Agile trace back to Toyota. PDCA, A3, and the TBP problem-solving approach are examples. These terms, which have made it into Agile and Agile Kata vocabulary, have their roots in the Toyota Production System. During a five-year research period between

2004 and 2009 that led to the book *Toyota Kata*, Mike Rother wanted to find answers to two major research questions:

- What are the unseen managerial routines and thinking that lie behind Toyota's success with continuous improvement and adaption?

- How can other companies develop similar routines and thinking in their organization?

The key word in the first question, in my opinion, is *unseen*. There are a lot of visible things you notice in organizations—frameworks, tools, and processes like Scrum, Kanban, A3, and Extreme Programming, just to name a few. There are also a ton of product tools that are visible in forms of dashboards, plans, and other artifacts.

Should you visit a Toyota plant as a guest, you might wonder why Toyota is so public and transparent about how they build their products. Why would they not treat their facility like the best-kept secret and secure it like Fort Knox? The reason is that you can easily observe the production process with your eyes, but problem-solving techniques are not as easy to recognize. It's difficult to see the underlying pattern that defines the culture of the organization by simply visiting a manufacturing plant, but the results of rigorous continuous improvement with kata, however, are visible.

When visitors return to their parent company after a tour at Toyota, they can share their findings and observations, based on what was visible to them. However, the pattern of creating a continuous improvement culture would not have been overt because the continuous improvement *is* the culture rather than the tools and processes that emerge. Scrum, Kanban, or Extreme Programming might be the process of choice in an organization, but the culture is about agility instead of a specific process or framework. I have seen many teams and organizations switch from one process to another as they are aiming for increasing agility.

If you decide to copy the approach of another company, you will copy the visible elements but not the culture. In my opinion, it's not surprising that so many organizations that have tried to copy the so-called Spotify model have not achieved the same culture within their organization. The interesting fact about the Spotify model is that not even Spotify follows it. A depiction of a model is outdated the moment it's finally captured because the culture has already evolved to something else. So when you look at the Spotify model that was created years ago, you can be certain that you would be copying something that is surely outdated and not even the current reality at Spotify.

At first, copying an existing model might seem like a good idea. For example, depicting a process framework or methodology in a fancy slide deck or poster and sharing it via email with the entire organization is fast but ineffective. How do you know the framework is applied as intended? I learned this the hard way during an Agile transformation at AOL in the early 2000s, where time was of the essence and we unfortunately did "kata corners" and shared models without the proper practice.

A picture might be worth a thousand words,[11] but it does not tell the whole story by itself. More importantly, the essence of the picture needs to be captured. Otherwise, you're just making a copy of a copy, and the desired culture slowly fades away. I know many Scrum teams that have colorful Scrum posters hanging at their walls, but what they're practicing on the ground has little to do with Scrum. There is a mismatch between desired and actual state. It's not unlike the practice of putting a flyer of the Dutch Reach in the glove compartment as I mentioned earlier. It is hard to expect real behavioral change from that.

With a kata mindset, you can create your own journey toward agility that fits your industry, expertise, and competitive landscape. With a kata mindset, you can create your own model, not on a company level like Spotify, but actually for each Agile team. Agility is not "installed" or "adopted." Transforming an organization is ongoing and continuous, and kata can be a pattern for that.

One reason we seem to crave simple solutions at work might be rooted in our brain trying to conserve energy. It's definitely more energy efficient to apply an existing model than to create a new one. Creating new neurological pathways, especially the super highways, requires more time to get stronger. It does not happen overnight.

Instead of asking, "What can we see as best practices that we want to install in our company?" you might ask, "What is our vision for success in our company, and what big challenges do we need to achieve to get there?" In the process of working on your own organization, you might get some ideas from other successful organizations. Those might become target conditions to experiment toward.

Another question to ask is why do people expect a copy-and-paste solution to be an appropriate tool in a highly innovative environment? How does "applying cookie-cutter solutions and pre-scriptive processes for knowledge work and creative product design" sound to you? Just copying someone else's success story does not mean that it will also be successful for you. Even if you do think it can work for you, by the time you have successfully copied it, your competitor that has a continuous improvement mindset is most likely another step ahead. With an approach like this, you will be in constant catch-up mode, and it will not reflect your unique culture and domain of your organization.

Any model needs to be validated continuously, or it becomes stale and obsolete. From your experience, how many playbooks and diagrams have you seen in your company that depict something different than what is happening on the ground? Leaders looking at these models will easily get the wrong impression about what is going in their organization. It might give people an inappropriate sense of comfort and achievement in a transformation. If they instead do a gemba walk, which refers to a practice in Lean management and means *visiting the real place*, the leaders will be connected directly with the people doing the work and the obstacles

---

11.   https://en.wikipedia.org/wiki/A_picture_is_worth_a_thousand_words

and impediments they are experiencing. A gemba walk is part of an open, transparent organizational culture that enables trust and a platform for further continuous improvement.

With Agile Kata, you can create your own way of working and create a model your competitors will envy you for. Although it is more time-consuming than copying someone else's approach, it has a real chance for effective organizational and cultural change, and it's what Spotify coaches recommend when they tour the world and share their experiences in conferences.

With Agile Kata, you have a pattern to improve your team's agility, adapt your product to new market conditions, and innovate to follow or lead others. The kata can be your continuous improvement pattern to steer agile transformations and so much more, as you will see in the rest of this book.

The kata offers many opportunities because it's a simple and universal pattern. It's easy to explain, so first let's take a look at Improvement Kata and Coaching Kata; they're at the core and foundation of Agile Kata. Then in Part II, we use that foundation to increase agility.

Reflection

- Reflect on a day at work and write down some of the habits that make up your day.

- Can you name an example where you have changed a routine behavior from your childhood for the better in your adult life?

- Try to think of a time when you made an ad hoc decision based on little evidence but were convinced it would work.

- Can you describe a situation where you thought you could easily perform, only to find it was harder than you initially thought?

- What was your last experiment at work that did not result in the desirable outcome?

- Can you describe a situation in your work environment where procedures and processes do not match the behavior of people performing the work?

2

Improvement Kata

To introduce Improvement Kata, I want to stick with the Dutch Reach example I introduced in the previous chapter. What is the actual sequence of steps that can make us change for good and start opening our car door in a better way? In Chapter 1, I argued that printing flyers and placing them into the glove compartment of each new car sold is not a promising idea. How about explaining the Dutch Reach in every driving school around the country? Better, I believe, but it's still a short-lived solution. So, how can we practice this new behavior? How about a sticker on the door handle as a constant reminder to use the other hand? We're entering the space of experimentation.

The same is true for any new habits for improvements. Studying footage of world-class tennis players does not necessarily mean that I will improve my tennis skills. During childhood, we have the urge to learn by doing. Holding a racket, comparing it with the image in front of us, and modeling how we hit a ball. This approach provides immediate feedback, so we can adjust and repeat.

In this chapter, I walk you through an actual kata pattern that can guide you through any change—playing tennis, losing weight, learning a new language, or opening a car door. These are all good candidates for applying the so-called Improvement Kata. The spectrum of examples for which you can use Improvement Kata gives you an idea on how universal the pattern is.

Step 1: Understand the Direction or Challenge

It all begins with a goal or direction. What is it you would like to achieve?

The first step of the four-step Improvement Kata reminds us to create a goal or rally around a given challenge (Figure 2.1). That goal is not time-bound, but it is recommended that you think about something that can be accomplished, let's say, in nine months or less. There aren't specific rules around the timeline. The important word is *can* because there is no guarantee that you will achieve the goal in the allotted time frame. As a matter of fact, you might not achieve the goal at all. This approach is very different from traditional management approaches where plans are being executed with an expectation of achieving the goal. In these traditional approaches, missing the goal is often considered failure. In the Improvement Kata, the challenge should feel bold and demanding, and it should release a burst of energy.

Figure 2.1
Understand the direction and challenge

The goal and direction of Improvement Kata describes a challenge that has a chance to be accomplished. You should feel motivated by a challenge—not bored or feeling paralyzed because it might be way out of reach. For example, in my opinion, starting a brand-new space traveling program and landing on the moon in six months' time does not seem realistic. A routine task that you have done multiple times before is not challenging enough. People also like context for decision-making. When challenges are unrealistic, it's impossible to get individuals or teams behind the idea to create momentum.

Addressing a challenge beyond nine months introduces additional problems, many that are related to being human. That's why I picked that timeline earlier. Staying focused and energized over a longer period of time is less likely than keeping focus for a short period. If the time box is too big, we might procrastinate due to a lack of urgency. It's also much harder to get a handle on very big challenges.

Associating a timeframe with the challenge is by no means a rule; it only serves as a general orientation when defining a challenge. It's not a failure in planning if you achieve the challenge in only three months or if you require additional time and reach it in a year. At the outset, the direction gave the individual or team a much-needed purpose and goal. It guided them through the process of reaching the goal. That is all that's necessary at that moment.

Big, massive goals aren't a bad idea. An organization has a big vision; it's not a problem. You can use that vision, which might span across several years, and use it as your North Star (or Southern Cross). You can break the long-term vision down into smaller chunks and use the pieces as challenges that then fit as that first step of Improvement Kata. That produces an achievable, realistic goal, which will serve the overarching vision. It will most likely result in many different kata across the organization, which will help maintain focus on both the smaller challenge at hand and the long-term vision.

For a 6-year old boy with the vision of becoming a professional tennis player, the first step of understanding the direction and challenge could be to learn fundamental forehand and backhand baseline hits. He might also put a measurable unit next to the direction and challenge, such as the number of successfully returned balls, either forehands or backhands, without causing any errors (net, miss, out of bounds, and so on).

Understanding the direction or challenge does not mean that you know how to achieve it or have an understanding about the tasks and exact path needed to get there. It just means that a person or team knows what we are trying to achieve. It's also absolutely normal that the challenge becomes clearer while you are working toward it. If you have a clear understanding that the goal will be achieved in the desirable time-window, your challenge is really not a challenge, and the path to get there is way too predictable. In this case, you would most likely be in the clear domain of the Cynefin framework.

Understanding the direction requires you to mentally step forward and think about the longer-term future. A well-defined challenge is the space between a "bore-out" and a "burn-out" syndrome. The in-between of these extremes is a great definition of a direction or challenge. The challenge should not be overwhelming but also not underwhelming.

Step 2: Grasp the Current Condition

Having a direction, challenge, or goal is great. It's helpful to have an idea where a journey could be going, but to really know where the journey is going and if it's a realistic endeavor, you need to first learn where you are currently are. The question is not about knowing the path to achieve the challenge, but to understand how big the overall gap between where you are and where you want to be is. There are no guarantees in life, and things are unpredictable, but a reference point is needed. For example, "landing on the moon in six months" had no reference to the current state of the space program. Are we making assumptions that the program is starting from scratch? What is the maturity of the program at that point? Is there sufficient funding? What is the experience of the team? We simply don't know.

Improvement Kata brings us mentally back into the present time. This second step is called Grasp the Current Condition (Figure 2.2).

Figure 2.2
Grasp the current condition

This is an important step in this scientific thinking pattern. Instead of jumping to conclusions, trying to solve a problem, and starting an initiative, grasping the current condition reminds everyone to step back and look carefully at the current situation. Don't kata corners!

During this step, you will try to gain a deep understanding of the process, problem, or challenge you are trying to solve. Observing the current process and performing a value stream mapping activity, for example, will help to collect data and insights about inefficiencies.

Mike Rother proposes a structured approach to grasp the current condition. He suggests learning with the body, for example in a gemba walk or genchi genbutsu, but also performing starter routines that make use of data and facts and recognizing any operating patterns. Learning and gathering facts provides a deeper understanding with no assumptions. Genchi genbutsu—which means to go and see yourself with no assumptions—and get the facts, underscores that importance. In Part II, I share examples of practices that can help you grasp a current condition for an Agile team.

Step 2 isn't easy, and some organizational cultures applaud behaviors of employees who immediately jump in and aim to fix things right away without fully grasping the current state of affairs. However, grasping the current condition is not a lengthy detour or time commitment. You can assess the starting point with a relatively short reflection period, and you'll ideally have some qualitative or quantitative evidence to assist you.

Grasping the current condition is a critical step in many ways. First, it gives you an opportunity to measure the delta between your current condition and the longer-term goal. How big is the desired change? Second, it gives you a starting point. One of the benefits of applying Improvement Kata is that it is not a start-to-end process. Grasping the current condition can start anywhere in your journey. I go into much more detail later in this book; for now, think about the various states organizations are in regarding their Agile transformation or their level of business agility. Improvement Kata can start anywhere in your journey and help you improve, regardless of how much progress you have made already. This step is a very appealing part of Agile Kata because not only are the world's problems diverse, but company cultures are as well.

Grasping the current condition is a very typical step in the realm of learning. Think about tryouts for sports teams or a school selection system. For the tennis example I used earlier, the boy could be totally new to the sport of tennis. He might not know how to hold a racket or successfully swing forehand or backhand. As a result, he can't get a ball over the net from the baseline successfully. Other players may have a different level of expertise due to possible previous tennis experiences. That is exactly the power of Improvement Kata. It applies to all levels and all situations and shows that it's truly a universal approach.

From a timeline perspective, grasping the current condition brings you back to the present and where you currently are in your journey.

Step 3: Establish the Next Target Condition

With an understanding of the direction and having a better grasp on the current condition, defining a small step forward is a logical third step in the pattern sequence. Step 3 is called Establish the Next Target Condition (Figure 2.3). In contrast to Step 1, which can give us direction for the next six to nine months, the target condition represents one step in that direction.

Figure 2.3
Establish the next target condition

When I delivered object-oriented analysis and design courses in the early 2000s, there was a concept of so-called operational contracts. Operational contracts describe two pictures: a picture from before an event occurred and a picture after the event occurred. The picture before is the current condition, whereas the picture after represents the target condition. The technique described only what the differences are, not how to implement them.

This step is not a detailed plan to get from the current condition to the target condition but a picture of what the small step forward could look like. The target condition is not a list of tasks or work assignments. It describes a desired state. How you get there is not important at this point. Therefore, planning multiple target conditions ahead of time is not a good idea either. You take one step at a time. It's like walking with a flashlight in the dark. With every step taken, more new information about the territory becomes visible. As the focal point, the target condition offers a clear vision of what success may look like.

For example, a next target condition criterion in the tennis example might be the ability to hit five straight forehands over the net. To make the target more concrete, the goal is to hit the ball straight on; additional complexities of top spin or slice aren't in the equation for now. Backhand shots aren't included, which creates additional focus on the target.

If you're familiar with Scrum or other iterative processes, you might think of a time-boxed sprint or iteration here. The target condition is different, though; it's not time-boxed, per se. In

Improvement Kata, you're not planning where you'd like to be two or three weeks from now; you're describing the condition of your next target. It doesn't matter whether you achieve that target in three days, one week, or exactly 2 weeks.

If you like, you can add a so-called "achieve-by" date to the next target condition. This can serve as a reminder on your calendar to reflect on the progress you made toward the target condition. You can then decide whether you need more time or to redesign the approach.

I can imagine an abundance of reasons why a target condition might not have been reached. One reason could be that the target condition was too aggressive. Another one is that the achieve-by date was too aggressive or that the experiments were not effective. In these cases, the target condition could be replaced, the achieve-by date extended, or ideas for new experiments brainstormed.

For everyone familiar with iterative processes, the achieve-by date is not a time-box, and the goal is not to fill allotted time with work. The achieve-by date is a checkpoint and reality check.

If the achieve-by date is set because of seasonal goals, like a Black Friday sales event or year-end closing procedures, the achieve-by date is more time relevant.

Should you achieve the target before the achieve-by date, the need for reflection is no longer needed, and it can be removed from the calendar.

The next target condition is a small step forward from your current condition. Mentally, you're stepping forward into the near future.

Step 4: Experiment Toward the Target Condition

The fourth and final step of Improvement Kata is to bridge the gap between the current condition and the target condition. This is done by organizing one or more experiments (Figure 2.4). Please remember that the current condition and the target condition are states. They are not a plan of actions and tasks to be accomplished to get there.

Once the current and target conditions are defined, a person or team executes a series of experiments. Instead of trying many things at once, it is recommended to take one idea, or one experiment, at a time. Please note that the result of an experiment is unknown. You're defining a hypothesis to test by trying it. An experiment where you know the outcome beforehand is not an experiment.

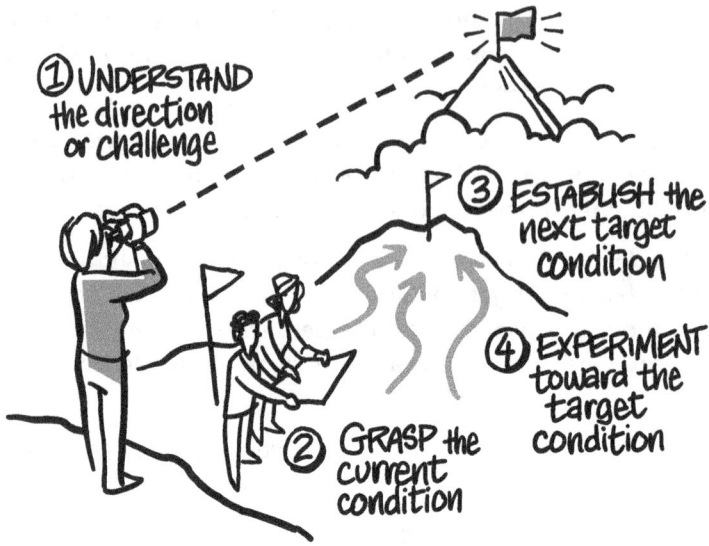

Figure 2.4
Experiment toward the target condition

After each experiment, you do not need to do advanced statistical analysis; instead, you simply ask "what happened?" and "what did I learn?" The arrows around Step 4 illustrate the continuous and iterative focus during experimentation. Additionally, you may have noticed in Figure 2.4 that there are many possible paths between the current and target conditions. Regardless of which one you're taking, expect the path to be bumpy. To foster a culture of scientific thinking, you tackle one experiment at a time so that the results don't become blurry and have unwanted side effects on other experiments. Combining experiments makes it much more difficult to measure the effectiveness of each individual experiment alone.

The pattern of Improvement Kata brings innovative and creative ideas to the surface. If you take the plan of actions away entirely and only define the next state, a group can easily self-organize around a given problem and create a series of possible experiments that aren't planned upfront but unfold over time. Once an experiment brings you to the target condition, the next target is defined. That said, even if one of the experiments leads to the target, it does not necessarily mean that a team will stop experimenting. There could be other opportunities to explore that might promise an even better outcome. You don't plan a future target condition before the prior one has been achieved because you would not have acquired the knowledge to inform any future target. Each target informs the next and may change the direction you're heading in.

Experimenting Example

A financial institution in New York tried something in the late 2000s that I had not seen in the IT domain before. They had a very complex problem to solve and brought in three different consultancies to tackle the same problem. All three companies got three months' time before they were asked to return and show their approach. The three companies did not know of each other, but they knew that only one of the three would get the contract to build out the rest of the solution. All three got paid for the first three months.

Two consultancies still worked a traditional waterfall approach at that time and took the specification and disappeared for three months. The third consultancy asked the client for a point of contact and a checkpoint meeting every two weeks. You can probably guess who got the contract at the end, but that is of less importance right now. Instead, think about all the possible avenues to a target condition. A team might keep exploring for better ways, even though they have already reached the target. But multiple teams[1] could also explore in parallel to bring out the best innovation and creativity. Those teams could be internal or external.

Not Reaching the Target Condition

What if there is no traction in any of the experiments taken? That is where the achieve-by date comes into the mix. The achieve-by date is the safety net that protects a team from experimenting too long without any tangible results. In this case, I suggest revisiting the validity or scope of the target condition and going back to the drawing board.

There are no rules or specific behaviors that need to be followed for experiments or the achieve-by date. Like with the entire kata mindset, common sense should rule and guide you. For example, if a person in a team has another creative idea for an experiment even though the achieve-by date has just been reached, it is perfectly OK for a team to give it a try. There is no time-box rule.

Learning from Experiments

Whether an experiment is successful or unsuccessful, the goal is to learn from each one and apply what you've learned to your subsequent experiments.

Returning one more time to the tennis example, the experiments to learn a good forehand hit from the baseline could be watching online videos, purchasing an online training guide, consulting a book or friend who knows how to play, or hiring a coach. There are many other possibilities as well. In terms of tools to support the experiments, you could buy beginner-level foam balls, rent a ball machine, record videos, and so on. Most importantly, stepping on a tennis court and practicing becomes essential. One thing is for certain: the boy will not learn to play tennis by observation. He will need to get on a court and hit a ball at some point. The earlier someone does that, the better.

Each experiment is designed in a way that will move you into the direction of the target condition, but there is no guarantee that it will do that. After the experiment has been executed, you would see if you were right. This might seem obvious, but in many organizations I have worked

---

1. Toyota's SBCE (Set-Based Concurrent Engineering)

with, goals and targets existed, but teams often worked involuntarily on other activities that were not serving the goal. If you don't focus on the target condition when you create an experiment, you will never achieve the target condition.

You could envision what you think the result would look like by asking, "What do I expect will happen?"

The target condition needs to be shared and understood, and then experiments can be planned. Planning includes building a hypothesis and envisioning what the result could look like. When you can ask, "What do I expect will happen?" you would look at the target condition and, if needed, break the smaller goal into a series of steps. Then for each step, you would design success criteria or a hypothesis so you know when the goal has been achieved. Again, facts are friendly.

Motivation for Experiments

Having an idea and using experiments solely to validate the idea is not in line with scientific thinking. Experimenting with the goal of eliminating waste is also not a good idea. This goal is not inspirational enough to carry someone with enough energy for a longer period of time. A more promising approach is identifying opportunities for improvements by using a value stream mapping exercise and then tying them to kata.

The urgency for experiments changes drastically when you shift the question from "What can we improve?" to "What do we need to improve?" The second question requires a goal and, with the goal, changes the approach for conducting the experiments. It also reminds everyone that there are a ton of things that *can be* improved, but there are some essential ones that *need to be* improved. It makes you think more holistically and focus on a business need rather than just looking at an isolated improvement idea.

Reflecting After an Experiment

After each experiment, it's a good practice to learn and adapt by analyzing the results and gathering insights. Are you closer to the target condition? What did you learn? Based on the findings, you either refine or abandon the current experiment and plan the next experiment. You may also realize your direction needs to change.

Don't think of an experiment necessarily as being this big breakthrough moment each time. They could be very small adjustments in behavior or work. The important part of experiments is that the result and outcome of them is unknown before you start. You test and compare the results against the target after the experiments are conducted. The beauty is that experimentations help eliminate assumptions and bias. By doing experiments, you avoid risky big-planned changes by working iteratively and in smaller batches with the necessary inspection and adaptation during and after each experiment.

Just before you begin your experiments, the gap in the path between the current condition and target condition is the widest. At this point, you know *what* the current condition is and *what* the target condition is but not *how* to navigate to the target condition—yet. Each experiment or step toward the target condition will make it clearer over time.

Imagine you are standing in a dimly lit room, and you find it challenging to see the details of an object across the room. As you take a step toward the object, the distance between you and the object decreases, and your perspective changes. By getting closer, the object appears larger, and you can detect more details and features that were previously obscured. Your improved visibility enables you to better understand the object's characteristics and identify specific attributes that were not apparent from a distance. It shows that even small changes, like taking a step forward, can lead to significant improvements not only about the object you observe but also the surroundings. You might even realize that the assumption of what kind of object you perceived in the beginning was entirely wrong. For example, a snake on the ground in the far distance may turn out to be a harmless stick as you get closer to it.

The point where visibility is limited and vision is blurry is called the learning edge or the current knowledge threshold (Figure 2.5). The learning edge is not a static fixed event. It moves along with you in your journey. As you learn more over time (stepping forward), the learning edge changes to a new location. This stepwise process of experimentation continues until the target condition is reached. The ability to recognize the learning edge and knowledge threshold is something that comes with experience. When you cross over the learning edge into the zone of unpredictability and uncertainty, words you use become vague and soft. For example, "I believe all teams have been trained in agile processes," or "last year 90 percent of the employees learned the Agile fundamentals." Facts are friendly, but data needs to be up to date to be relevant.

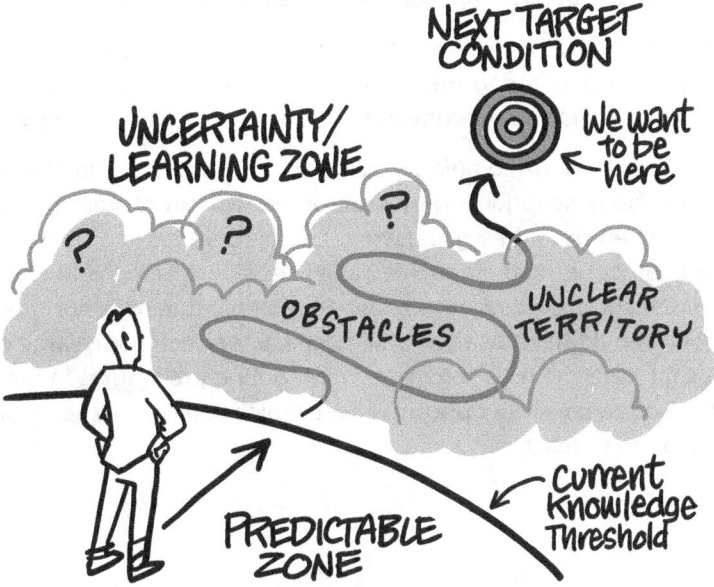

Figure 2.5
The learning edge, predictable zone, and learning zone (Adapted from The Toyota Kata Practice Guide *by Mike Rother.)*

Activity: 15-Minute Learning Edge Daily Challenge

1. Set a daily topic.

2. Find reliable resources (5 minutes).

3. Learn something new about the topic (5 minutes).

4. Reflect on your learning.

5. Apply or share your learning.

6. Keep a journal.

Learn something new and push yourself from the comfort zone to the learning zone in this daily activity. Ideally, you will apply the newly learned skill at work or in your daily life. Share what you've learned with a friend or colleague. Sharing your findings with someone else, in your own words, reinforces your learning tremendously. Keep a log of your topic, insights, and learning journey, and you will see how the learning edge changes over time.

When leaving the comfort zone, where someone would perform routine activities with their existing skills and knowledge, some people feel discomfort due to potential failure. However, being in the comfort zone means that someone is not being challenged and has little potential for personal and professional growth. Wayne Gretzky's quote "You miss 100 percent of the shots you don't take" is a reminder of how important it is to leave the comfort zone.

The learning zone is also known as the growth zone, where people expand their skills through new experiences. Individuals entering this learning zone need to trust that to the rest of the organization, including leaders and executives, failure is seen as a learning opportunity.

Steven Spear, who coined the term *zombie organization*,[2] refers to individuals who try to do their job according to their job description. When confronted with an obstacle, they try to remove the obstacle in a way to return to their given work. Zombie cultures in organizations show signs of fire fights and workarounds, rigid hierarchies, slow decision-making, and an inability to learn from mistakes. It's fascinating to point out that when multiple threats occur simultaneously in a zombie organization, it could have a catastrophic impact. I've seen many large organizations in situations like this that have the urge to create more routine procedures in handbooks and so forth. Ironically, these often have the opposite effect, which could easily spiral and paralyze the culture of an organization to react.

---

2. [SS2010]

Contrary to a zombie organization is a *dynamic organization*, which is more adaptable and agile. A dynamic organization would embrace a culture of problem-solving. In a dynamic culture, side effects of problems are put into perspective as well. That way, a problem is solved for one part of an organization with other parts in mind. As a result, those problems do not cause a ripple effect later. A dynamic organization is constantly exploring the learning edge with the goal to push forward.

Underscoring this idea, a key finding in a report issued by the U.S. Secretary of Education in 1983 said, "educational reform should focus on the goal of creating a learning society." That is in sync with the other educational agencies around the world that have defined twenty-first-century skills. There is consensus on how our approach to work has shifted drastically in recent years. What used to be a hard management skill only a few years ago became a blocker in a transformation to a modern company. The 4C's—which stand for the core skills of critical thinking, communication, collaboration, and creativity—are a good example of that.

Improvement Kata as a whole and Step 4 in particular can enable a dynamic organization. Rapid cycles with frequent small experiments have an even bigger impact on the results.

One thing I have been doing in my learning talks is something I saw Mike Rother do during a conference as well. It's a great example for exploring the learning zone a little bit. Consider the following sequence. What do you think will follow 10?

> 2,4,6,8,10,?
> How about 12?

What is missing here is context. We don't have enough information to make a prediction. These are just numbers. Your first instinct might be 12, but what if the sequence came to an end with 10 and starts all over again with 2? Even though 12 seems to be logical at the beginning, with more context, 2 could also be a possible choice. Context is important, especially when you're at the learning edge. Context is the set of circumstances or facts that surround a particular situation or set of conditions—the organizational environment or landscape.

It might sound like a tedious effort, but kata professionals document their experiments and findings. It is recommended to log some information for each experiment, such as the date and what you expect to happen, what actually happened, and what you learned. One side is captured before the experiment, and the other side is recorded after the experiment. That experimentation record finds its way into one particular segment in the so-called storyboard, which supplements entire Improvement Kata.

Before we take a look at that next, let's revisit some kata terminology. Figure 2.6 has terms sandwiched between *vision* and *action*. Most importantly it shows how detailed and granular the items are becoming the closer you get to the actionable level.

Figure 2.6

From vision to action (Adapted from Vision to Action with the Improvement Kata *by Beth Carrington.)*

Whenever I introduce Improvement Kata to individuals, I get questions about the number sequence of the four steps. Take another look at Figure 2.4. Why is the sequence 2,4,3,1 and not 1,2,3,4? Sometimes people even hint to me that my slide has typos, which is not the case.

The timeline behind the stepping sequence is important. It should give the reader a sense of where they are in the pattern. For example, Step 1 is far in the future, far away from the present (Step 2). Then we make a small step into the future as the next target (Step 3) before we return to the present and run an experiment (Step 4).

If you prefer a more logical 1,2,3,4 sequence without the timeline, you can certainly think of Improvement Kata the way it is described in Figure 2.7.

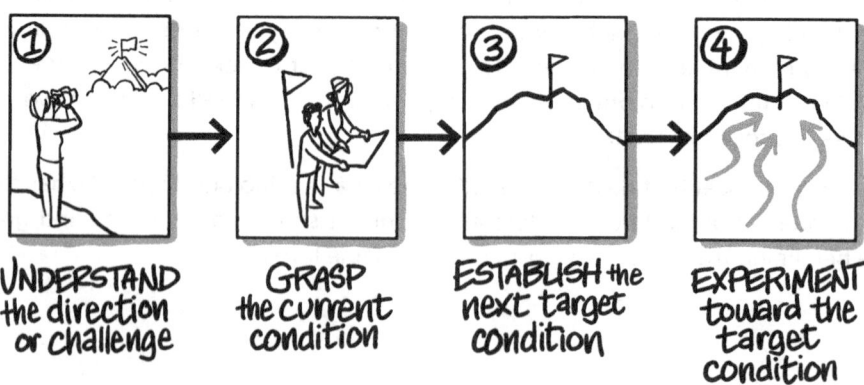

Figure 2.7

Improvement Kata with the 1,2,3,4 stepping sequence

Storyboard

A storyboard is a visual tool used to track the development of improvement activities that acts as an information dashboard to show the path from the current condition to the target condition over time. For teams currently using an agile process like Kanban or Scrum, the concept of visualizing progress on a physical or electronic board is not new.

When applying Improvement Kata, the storyboard becomes a visual tool for the person working on the improvement effort to get an orientation about the current state of work and experiments. It brings the current state of thinking back into the forefront of the learner.

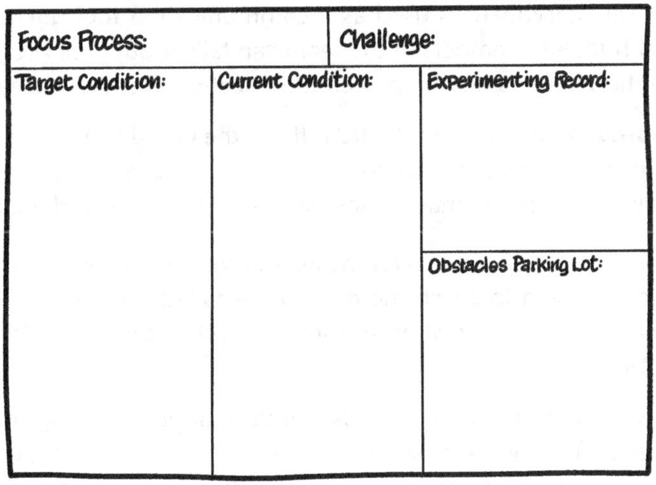

Focus Process:		Challenge:	
Target Condition:	Current Condition:	Experimenting Record:	
		Obstacles Parking Lot:	

Figure 2.8
Learner storyboard (Adapted from Learner Storyboard in The Toyota Kata Practice Guide *(2018) by Mike Rother.)*

You can see in Figure 2.8 that the sections on the board reflect the thought process of the four Improvement Kata steps. The challenge is captured visibly in the top-right corner of the board. The focus process serves as the larger scope context for orientation. This could be a reference to the targeted value stream in which the improvement takes place.

Below the section for challenge and focus process is a column on the left side describing the target condition. That often includes an optional achieve-by date. The state of the current condition is next to the target condition in the middle of the board.

On the far right are segments for listing the experiment record (a journal of planned and performed experiments) and a parking lot for obstacles.

When a learner, who is the person using Improvement Kata, is looking over the sections of the storyboard, it brings scientific thinking to the surface again. Ideally, if the storyboard is constantly present and visible next to the learner, the storyboard creates focus and commitment.

The benefits of a storyboard include the following:

- **Visualization:** A storyboard enables teams and individuals to depict their improvement initiatives visually, making it simpler to comprehend the actions taken and stay focused on the existing and desired situation. It offers a concise and straightforward up-to-date summary of the progress.

- **Transparency:** The storyboard encourages openness and visibility of the improvement activity. It helps everyone involved in the improvement effort, including team members, leaders, and stakeholders, to be on the same page and understand the progress being made.

- **Facilitation:** The storyboard is used as a communication tool during daily meetings or improvement huddles. Members of the team can talk about their progress, problems, and potential solutions, encouraging open communication and idea exchange.

- **Iterative improvement:** The storyboard reflects the iterative nature of Improvement Kata as the individual or team completes experiments and makes progress. It enables everyone to record their learnings and make plans for the next step toward the desired condition.

A storyboard can be thought of as a kata for the learner to summarize their thinking in a way that makes it visible for the coach to coach them. They are called "starter kata." It is not necessarily something you will use forever, but when starting to practice the kata, it is a powerful aid. It's a scaffolding for learning.

Other tools, such as Scrum or Kanban boards, are very popular among Agile teams. The kata storyboard is powerful when working with teams, which we will explore in more detail in Part II of this book. But the kata storyboard is also useful when working alone because it puts the current progress and context from the Improvement Kata directly in front of you.

I'm a big fan of physical boards. I have boards standing in my office. For individual learners, I highly recommend a physical board. If team members are collocated and share a space, a physical board is very powerful as well. Hybrid teams and remote teams probably benefit more from a digital version. Although the storyboard is not mandatory, I strongly recommend it as a valuable visual tool to support the improvement process.

The Storyboard not only provides a centralized location of information relevant to conduct Improvement Kata, but it is also flexible and adjustable. Take the storyboard as a starting point and evolve into something that fits your style and environment. Later in this book, when I discuss how Improvement Kata can be used with agility in mind, I explain how to take the basic storyboard template and modify it to work in the Agile context.

Storyboards are not only useful artifacts for the individual or teams. They can also support

- **Coaches:** May ask targeted questions about the Improvement Kata that were triggered by the latest content on the board.

- **Stakeholders:** Could be interested in the development and results of the improvement efforts even though they are not directly involved in the day-to-day improvement activities. To gain perspective on the team's work, offer feedback, and assist the team's efforts, they may periodically review the storyboard.

- **Leaders/managers:** Can comprehend ongoing improvement initiatives, provide resources, and align improvement efforts with overarching organizational goals.

- **Subject matter experts:** May interact with the storyboard to share insights, collaborate, or contribute to particular experiments, depending on the structure of the organization and the nature of the improvement effort.

Regardless of your specific approach to the storyboard and its audience, the key is to follow Improvement Kata's fundamental principles and practices. The storyboard is not the Improvement Kata but just a visual representation of the current Improvement Kata actions.

An elaborately designed storyboard does not necessarily make your Improvement Kata better. Don't overthink or overengineer the board. The goal is to achieve lasting improvement and create a culture of continuous learning and progress. A Storyboard that is static and only sits in a corner without anyone working with it is a waste of time. Use and adjust your storyboard over time so it makes sense for you and your team.

Reflection

- What would be an improvement idea in your personal or professional life that could be a good candidate for Improvement Kata?

- Do you remember a life situation in which you applied Improvement Kata without even realizing it?

- Can you name a situation where work was completed faster than anticipated or vice versa?

- What drives you personally to pursue any goal?

- What tools of visualization do you use during the day?

- Can you name a large goal in your work environment and define a small goal that could be a stepping stone to get there?

3

Coaching Kata

Improvement Kata, which is introduced in the previous chapter, is a general pattern to potentially improve anything. You can use Improvement Kata for countless things—for example, starting a healthier lifestyle, learning a new language or instrument, or becoming a better athlete.

Performing Improvement Kata by yourself in isolation is not for everybody. Some people need additional motivation to produce an environment of continuous improvement. For example, think about a time in your life when you had a big New Year's resolution, but your energy and focus for keeping it faded away after only a few weeks.

So why not use a coach like so many do in music, learning, arts, or sports? Coaching is such a typical thing in these fields that it's surprising that the business world has also not fully embraced it. People who do take advantage of coaching often quickly learn how powerful it is.

Let's take a look at a different kata that complements Improvement Kata by adding a coaching stance. Appropriately it is called Coaching Kata.

The Coach

Coaching Kata consists of two roles: a coach and a learner. What does this relationship look like? By default, the coach works in a 1:1 relationship with the learner, and ideally they meet for a short time every day. A rule of thumb is 20 minutes a day, but after the initial stages of setting up a project, the time may be much shorter than that on some days—perhaps even only 5 minutes.

During this time, the learner reflects on their goals, targets, and experiments by examining the content on the storyboard (Figure 3.1). The first goal of the coach is to help the learner apply and practice the Improvement Kata steps. That means the coach has been in the role of a learner before and has experienced Improvement Kata and gained practice with it firsthand.

At Toyota manufacturing, there is a supervisor/subordinate relationship between the learner and the coach, and that relationship is based on their rank or seniority. Later in this book, we break that traditional relationship when we apply the kata mindset for self-organized teams. For now, think of the coach as a person who may or may not have knowledge and experience in the business domain as well as Improvement Kata itself.

Figure 3.1
Coaching cycle with learner and coach in front of a storyboard

The learner and coach play significantly different roles, but they are both learning in their own ways during the coaching cycle. When a learner admits to not knowing something—an admission that isn't easy to make—those words should trigger a coaching moment. Rather than directing the learner, the coach uses questions to guide them in finding answers. That creates an environment for critical thinking and ownership of problem-solving. At Toyota, failure is seen as an opportunity to learn rather than a situation to be avoid. Where there are problems, there could be failures. Taiichi Ohno, one of the founding fathers of the production system, said, "Having no problems is the biggest problem of all."[1]

A way the coaching model at Toyota is fundamentally different from others is that coaching is integrated into the workplace. The learner is coached on the job. (It is known as OJD, or on-the-job development.) The saying "If the learner hasn't learned, then the teacher hasn't taught" defines nicely who the coach is: a teacher. We will explore these stances more in Chapter 6.

In Chapter 2, I used an example of tennis. Let me take you back to that one more time. If you want to improve your tennis skills, where would you go? A golf or soccer coach? Most likely not, I would assume. Why would anyone seek advice in a sport from somebody who does not know how to play the game? You look for expertise in the sport from someone who knows what they are talking about. In most cases, the coach is expected to be better in the discipline than the learner. In kata, a successful coach/learner relationship requires an experienced coach that coaches the learner in applying Improvement Kata.

So, what is Coaching Kata? It's a series of targeted, thought-provoking questions that the coach asks the learner during the daily coaching cycle. The coach does not try to solve the problem but helps the learner gain insights and understandings about the current situation.

Not only does Coaching Kata help the learner navigate through Improvement Kata, it helps the coach sharpen their own coaching skills. In a coach/learner relationship, both roles are learning. In situations where the coach has just transitioned from being a learner, there is a starter kata to begin the cycle, and it consists of five questions.

At first, it is recommended you simply read the questions out loud rather than improvising. There is no element of surprise expected by the learner, especially in the beginning of a coaching relationship. This helps the learner stay focused on the most important elements in the beginning. It also helps the coach in transitioning from learner through deliberate practice. As the coach gains experience, they will learn to ask deeper questions and ultimately develop their own coaching method.

The five starter kata questions for the coach are the following:

1. What is the target condition?

2. What is the actual condition now?

3. What are the obstacles you are addressing now?

4. What do you expect from your next step?

5. How quickly can we go and see what we have improved?

When asked, the learner reflects on the information on the storyboard, ideally in front it. This helps to synchronize the information on the board with what actually happened. Possible discrepancies are fixed on the spot.

1.　[TO1988]

As you can tell from these questions, each one brings the learner to a different segment on the storyboard. Technically, you could ask these questions in any order, but if you are new to Coaching Kata, I recommend asking them in the order they're on the storyboard. Once you become more comfortable with the role of kata coach and the questions, you will most likely begin asking follow-up questions. You might even give your own personal spin to any of the five questions. Whatever you do, it's most important to stay away from leading questions.

The Second Coach

Over time, a kata mindset creates an environment for continuous learning, improvement, and growth across an entire organization. This brings up a pressing question about the role of the coach. How does the coach learn, improve, and grow? Who is giving the coach feedback? To address that need, Coaching Kata uses the concept of a so-called second coach. That does not mean a second coach for the learner but a coach for the coach (Figure 3.2).

Figure 3.2
Coaching cycle with second coach

The second coach acts as an example of good coaching behaviors and techniques and aids the primary coach in honing their coaching skills and style by demonstrating effective coaching methods and strategies.

The second coach observes the interactions between the learner and the primary coach during coaching sessions and offers the primary coach constructive criticism, points out their strengths, and suggests areas for development. This feedback happens after the coaching cycle between the coach and learner, not while it's happening. The primary coach can improve their coaching techniques and become more successful in directing the learner with the help of this feedback.

Coaching can be difficult, especially for those who are just starting out. The second coach promotes a supportive and helpful coaching environment and provides encouragement to the primary coach. The second coach helps ensure that the coaching procedure adheres to the values and principles of Improvement Kata and Coaching Kata. They also provide feedback about the steps of Improvement Kata, including the experiments and whether the coaching questions were asked in an effective manner.

The coaching relationship is advantageous to the second coach as well. The secondary coach has the chance to expand their coaching abilities by watching the primary coach's interactions with the learner.

When a primary coach is new to Coaching Kata or is coaching complex improvement challenges, the presence of a second coach is especially helpful. It promotes a culture of ongoing learning and improvement among both coaches, while helping to maintain a structured and efficient coaching process.

Learner, coach, and second coach are all roles; they are not permanent positions or assignments. The relationship between the primary coach and the secondary coach might be flipped during a separate or parallel kata. In this case, both coaches would execute the role of a primary coach and secondary coach and mirror each other. This situation can be particularly effective for teams and organizations that are new to the kata mindset by accelerating the adoption of Improvement and Coaching Kata.

Reflection

- As a learner, what qualities are you looking for in a coach to help you be more effective as a learner?

- Can you describe a work situation where you would have benefited from a coach? If so, which one, why, and how?

- What areas of improvements do you see for yourself to become a kata coach?

- How could Improvement Kata steps help you become a better coach?

- Who is a person in your personal or professional environment who could become a second coach for you?

- Describe one small step that you can take to become a second coach to the Kata coaches.

PART II

AGILE KATA

Agile Kata is a universal pattern for continuously improving agility in organizations and teams.

Agile Kata can help you navigate your way to a wide range of challenging goals. You will see that the sky can truly be the limit. To illustrate this range, I have a few use cases in Part III. Those use cases will give you an idea of what is possible and how you can apply Agile Kata yourself.

But before you get to those, it is important you understand what Agile Kata is.

In Part I, I describe Improvement Kata and Coaching Kata, two simple routines to get you started. You can develop kata for learning any skill, and, in this case, the focus is scientific thinking. Kata is about breaking down a difficult skill, like karate, into small pieces and then through deliberate practice developing the habits needed to perform each kata naturally. Improvement Kata has a clear pattern of 1) defining the challenge, 2) understanding the current condition, 3) defining the next target condition, and 4) experimenting your way to each target condition on the way to the challenge. The routines have been developed to practice each of these steps, so they begin to feel natural.

Kata translates to *way of doing*; therefore, Agile Kata stands for *way of doing Agile*. This informs our way of being agile by applying scientific thinking skills with and for a team and not just an individual. You design experiments as a team and reach a challenge and targets through agility. It also means that teams are working in self-organized and self-managed ways, and leaders lead by serving, not directing. Working in agile ways means that you have tools and practices that help you transition to greater agility, but what is agility in the first place?

A definition and common understanding of Agile is important. I cover that in Chapter 4.

Working in agile ways means working in teams. Agile professionals typically do not work in isolation. And because we can use Kata to deliberately practice new habits, we use techniques that work well with the definition of Agile and with groups. We use the kata pattern, incorporating the practices, tools, and techniques and making them a new habit over time.

Coaching Kata parallels Improvement Kata and focuses on scientific thinking, which means it's very specific in a sense. However, the general approach to coaching by asking questions, supporting learners, and focusing on the process more than the content prepares the coach for more general types of facilitation because Agile teams are self-managed and autonomous. There are a variety of facilitation skills to keep the team focused, manage any conflicts that occur, and come to joint decisions and a variety of facilitation skills needed to complement Coaching Kata. I have several techniques and will show you how to integrate them in Agile Kata.

Coaching is not new to Agile teams, but what is the impact and what are the opportunities of the role of an Agile coach? How can a coach foster a culture of continuous improvement, scientific thinking, and agility?

Agile organizations are obsessed with finding ways to deliver value frequently and early. But how is value defined and how can you measure it? How can you truly listen and understand the voice of the customer rather than make assumptions about what they "must want"?

Scientific thinking focuses on the actual condition, testing ideas deliberately, and adjusting based on rapid feedback. How can you coach your teams in ways that respect their autonomy while encouraging true collaboration? How can you create a leadership culture that has the grit to systematically pursue any goal, even the seemingly impossible?

My goal is to provide answers to these questions by translating them into separate chapters in Part II. If you are an experienced Agile coach, you're probably already familiar with some of the techniques described here. Keep in mind that the goal is not to introduce and explain each of them but to show how you can work with them when performing Agile Kata. If they are new to you, the following chapters should give you enough information to evaluate the techniques. If you want to incorporate them, I provide references in the back of the book for you to explore further.

The chapters in Part II are

- "Agile as Values and Principles"
- "Measuring Value"
- "Agile Coaching"
- "Collaboration"
- "Leadership and Culture"

As you practice the skills of scientific thinking in your pursuit of continuous improvement, you will discover a new life for Agile methods. Too often the Agile landscape is dominated by standard frameworks and specific tools. For years, companies went through time-consuming and costly adoptions of Agile processes. When they face obstacles, I have seen them abandon ship and try something new. This feels like trying one fad diet after the next as you hope for that long-lasting break-through miracle moment. Hope is not a good strategy! Asking difficult questions to find out why things are not working with the existing frameworks and improve them continuously is much more promising. Have you seen teams switch from Scrum to Kanban, or vice versa, only to find out that the grass isn't always greener on the other side?

The Agile Kata takes a different approach. It can tackle your challenges head on when you are ready to practice change. Instead of seeing the process framework itself as a static structure, it challenges existing norms and rules. In countless conversations with executives, I heard statements like, "Things seem better since the introduction of *<name your method>*." However, is better enough, and how do you measure *better*? Agile Kata uses evidence and facts to move toward measurable goals.

This new way of thinking can take you beyond the existing frameworks and can shape something over time that works for you and your team. The beautiful thing is that you can start wherever you currently are in your transformation journey.

Blindly using methods for the sake of methods is as futile as blindly trying to copy another successful company. Spotify began its Agile journey with pure Scrum and followed it according to the Scrum Guide. Over time, the people at Spotify challenged the rules and made it work in their environment. It became the Spotify model, and many coaches and executives tried to cut and paste these as best practices. It's a hard realization to learn that what works for Spotify does not necessarily work for others. Spotify coaches always pointed out that the model grew with the growth of the company. Copying any model is just like copying a framework. You can't copy the underlying culture; you have to build it yourself. Have you noticed that agility is much more than adopting a framework, tool, or somebody else's success story? The irony, and an important realization, is that not even Spotify uses the "Spotify model." It was just a snapshot that captured how they worked at that moment in time.

Of course, using frameworks isn't a bad idea. They can be very helpful and serve as a starting point for Agile Kata. They can also be a source for inspiration for experiments. But using a framework that has worked for another organization doesn't mean you're going to see the same results.

When I began using kata to help Agile organizations improve, it raised certain questions: How does scientific thinking apply to working in teams? How can it be used to continuously improve agility? What is the impact on the role of an Agile coach? How can self-managed teams benefit from scientific thinking and the kata routine? What can agile leaders do to enable scientific thinking across the organization? How can kata positively impact an Agile culture? How does the focus on delivering value in Agile organizations align with scientific thinking? I share answers to these questions in the second part.

There are many existing tools, techniques, and practices that Agile teams use on a daily basis. Some of them are well known, proven, and documented. I picked a few of those and give them a spotlight for how you can use them in at least one of the four steps of the kata pattern.

Will Agile be a thing in the future? Change is the only constant in our complex world. Nobody can predict exactly what will happen in the future. There is a trend that the business world will be exposed to more VUCA[1], not less. And because Agile processes thrive in a VUCA world, I see a bright future of scientific thinking, continuous improvement, and the Agile Kata.

---

1.   Volatility, Uncertainty, Complexity and Ambiguity (https://en.wikipedia.org/wiki/VUCA)

4

Agile as Values and Principles

The Agile values and principles are defined in the Agile Manifesto. Agile is not a single specific start-to-end process or methodology. One way of looking at it is as a mindset. A mindset translates into a certain behavior.

You might also see Agile as a general philosophy that serves us through guiding principles for decision-making. Germans have a wonderful word for it—*Weltanschauung* (perception or view of the world[1])—that encompasses various factors such as cultural background, beliefs, ethics, science, and so on. It guides everyone in their actions, thoughts, and understanding of existence. Your perception of the world never matches someone else's perception. Maybe close, but not identical. When Agile is viewed as a philosophy, the Agile values and principles will shift and shape our minds by interpretation of them. Because we're changing habits and learn as an individual, I use the word *mindset* throughout this book, but always remember, someone's mind should always be flexible, and never be set.

There are several concrete Agile processes, methods, and frameworks you can use to achieve that mindset of agility. These could be Scrum, Kanban, or extreme programming (XP), just to name a few. There is neither only one Agile process nor an end-state of agility.

Agile values and principles anchor our community of professionals by not only a name but also how we behave. They guide us to approach projects and products radically differently than how

---

1. https://en.wikipedia.org/wiki/Worldview

we have approached projects and products prior to the release of the Agile Manifesto where these values and principles are defined. The challenge is that after years and years of working in traditional ways, we needed to change our habits to try something different. The change to Agile processes hasn't been easy, and evidence shows many organizations were challenged.

Many Scrum trainers referred to the introduction of Scrum as shock therapy. Remove everything you are currently doing and replace it with Scrum. In many cases, that has been proven to be too much of a habit change at once. As a result, Scrum got "installed," but the cultural change did not follow fast enough. Many teams also felt that a given framework did not represent their way of working. Cultural change requires more time, more practice, and more experiments. Kata is a way of doing that.

You need to step away from the actual process frameworks, methodologies, and tools to see what *agile* actually means and separate that from Agile process frameworks, methodologies, and tools. Knowing your domain in the Cynefin framework is also helpful.

Definition of Agile

The word *agile* can be an adjective or noun. When looking at the word *agile* as an adjective, it is easy to compare it to synonyms like *nimble, adaptive, flexible,* or someone that thinks and understands quickly. That interpretation is from a regular dictionary and often what leaders, executives, and managers think of when becoming agile. This is a very agreeable definition. Who would openly admit in an organization that they are not flexible and do not think or act quickly?

Agile as a noun, on the other hand, follows the definition outlined in the "Manifesto for Agile Software Development."[2]

In the context of this book and the relationship to Agile Kata, I exclusively use the noun meaning, even when the word *agile* is written in lowercase in this book. This distinction is very important because I believe many misconceptions about the success and impact of Agile is related to that. For example, you may feel that an Agile transformation has stalled because teams aren't delivering faster or aren't able to change gears whenever needed. Agile teams, on the other hand, may feel very agile because they strive for technical excellence by focusing on quality. Managing expectations about the goals and opportunities is therefore highly recommended.

A Gallup survey demonstrates some of these misunderstandings. For example, "Everybody wants agility, everybody thinks they have it, nobody actually does." The survey concludes that only 18 percent of employees say their company is Agile.[3]

---

2.   www.agilemanifesto.org

3.   https://www.gallup.com/workplace/611675/search-agility.aspx

Agile Manifesto

The Agile values and principles are defined in the Agile Manifesto. Agile is not a single specific start-to-end process or methodology. It's a philosophy.

The Agile Manifesto[4] defines 4 values and 12 principles. That's pretty much it. But perhaps its simplicity is its power, both to understand and to adapt for different circumstances. Figure 4.1 shows what the four values are.

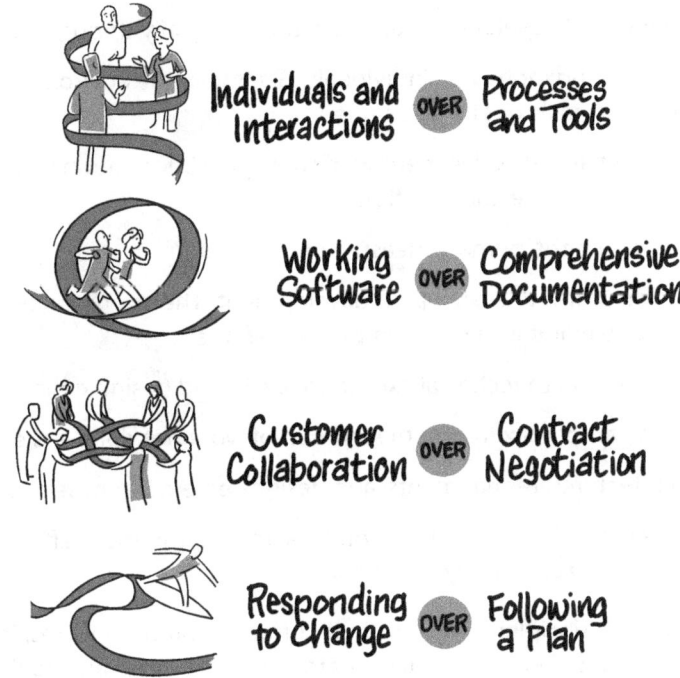

Figure 4.1
Agile value statements (text: Agile Manifesto; visual: Joe Krebs)

These values cut to the core of value-added for the customer. The customer is not interested in brilliant debate and analysis in our meetings. The customer does not care how colorful our kanban tickets are. They want products and services that work for them and help solve their daily problems. They want something that works seamlessly, is easy to use, is delivered on time, and is a good financial value.

If we were able to follow the four values, we would have teams continually developing working software, unencumbered by bureaucracy, with intensive customer interaction and feedback, adapting as they learned more. Who would not want that?

---

4. http://agilemanifesto.org/

We can get deeper into how to bring these values to life by looking at the 12 principles:

- Our highest priority is to satisfy the customer through early and continuous delivery of valuable software.

- Welcome changing requirements, even late in development. Agile processes harness change for the customer's competitive advantage.

- Deliver working software frequently, from a couple of weeks to a couple of months, with a preference to the shorter timescale.

- Business people and developers must work together daily throughout the project.

- Build projects around motivated individuals. Give them the environment and support they need, and trust them to get the job done.

- The most efficient and effective method of conveying information to and within a development team is face-to-face conversation.

- Working software is the primary measure of progress.

- Agile processes promote sustainable development. The sponsors, developers, and users should be able to maintain a constant pace indefinitely.

- Continuous attention to technical excellence and good design enhances agility.

- Simplicity—the art of maximizing the amount of work not done—is essential.

- The best architectures, requirements, and designs emerge from self-organizing teams.

- At regular intervals, the team reflects on how to become more effective, then tunes and adjusts its behavior accordingly.

Each time I read these principles, the word that comes to mind is *joy*. Yes, joy. Like many, I got into programming because I en-"joyed" it. It was my way of adding value to the world. As Richard Sheridan put it in his great book *Joy, Inc.: How We Built a Workplace People Love,*[5] it was my way of bringing "joy" to myself and others.

If I were part of an organization in my first job as a programmer that was acting out these principles, I would have found joy. We would have achieved the outcomes that the Gallop survey suggests companies want, and as employees painfully note, few companies achieve. As it turns out, few of us were part of such an organization, which drove us to want to do something and take action. And the actions taken in the name of Agile varied quite a bit.

I do not suggest that it would be easy or that the transformation could happen in a simple, linear fashion. Your position is not a black or white scenario. It is not about switching from one side to the other but how far your mindset has shifted toward the Agile values. That is true for

---

5.   [RS2015]

individuals but also the organization as a whole. That determines the level of agility, which is a gradual, continuous improvement process.

If we consider the four values, the desire of becoming agile requires a desire to continuously push the boundaries further and further (Figure 4.2). It is not a box to be checked, and there is no "mission accomplished" moment. As discouraging as this might sound for some, starting to introduce Agile means not having a clear, well-defined end state.

Figure 4.2
Agility as continuous improvement

The way the Agile Manifesto is written provides room for interpretation, which is a good thing. Every team situation is different and therefore requires a closer look at what is possible in its context. For example, larger organizations in a regulated and controlled environment will most likely interpret the Agile Manifesto differently than a small start-up. But both types of organizations will be pushing the boundaries of the Agile Manifesto toward the left side based on their current position and their opportunities. Agile Kata can be the vehicle for that. Making only one small step to the left then stopping and becoming complacent is not what we have in mind.

Driving Change Using the Agile Manifesto, Even Outside of IT

The full title of what is often referred to as the Agile Manifesto is actually "The Manifesto for Agile Software Development." When there are non-IT teams embracing Agile ways of working, the word *software* is often in their way. The translation to other domains can be difficult. To build that connection with teams outside of IT, the word *software* is often replaced with words like products, services, or whatever works best in your situation. The values and principles can stand; the actual words chosen might slightly differ.

The Agile Manifesto has given a community of software engineers a name and something to hold on to for decades. It serves as an important milestone. For professionals using Agile Kata, the Agile Manifesto can give initiatives, teams, and organizations a much-needed direction and guardrails. It's in the spirit of continuous improvement that some teams want to go beyond the values and principles we know today, which is desirable and to be encouraged. The idea that you may consider Agile Kata to shape the future of agility truly excites me.

When you parse the Agile Manifesto for words like *continuous*, you will find it twice. Searching for *iteration* or *timebox*? You won't find it even once. References like *frequently, at regular intervals, constant pace indefinitely*, or *must work together daily* show that the Agile Manifesto always fostered a mindset of flow, repetition, and continuation.

A construct like an iteration, found in Agile frameworks, is therefore not required to be agile. You can, and should, challenge existing rules, roles, and events if they don't make sense.

A team or organization can use the Agile Manifesto as guardrails for continuous improvement. Then the 12 principles become that philosophy I mentioned earlier and should be on your radar when you're going through organizational change. But sometimes we filter the ones we like or are familiar with and are biased in our view. Damn those habits again!

But what if you do use one of the 12 principles as your direction? Take "Business people and developers must work together daily throughout the project" as an example. That is definitely a possibility but has a drawback. Here's why:

Shouldn't you use Agile to solve a business problem? Becoming Agile is not the goal; solving the business problems you're facing within your organization is the goal. Becoming Agile helps you solve your business challenges, but that's not the main reason to start with Agile. That said, I am aware that many organizations want to become Agile without asking that pressing "why?" question first.

So here is a different approach: Your organization has identified "low customer engagement" as a bottleneck using value stream mapping or a technique of your choice. Now you have a clear business challenge to "increase customer engagement."

Using that challenge, you can connect the Agile principle "Deliver working software frequently, from a couple of weeks to a couple of months, with a preference to the shorter timescale" to the challenge.

Are you delivering working software frequently? If not, why not? You're now addressing a business challenge and using Agile principles as your guide. When you do that, you will quickly learn that it's quite common that more than one principle will impact your business challenge. In the example of "Increasing customer engagement," you can probably make a case for linking two more principles to the business challenge:

- Welcome changing requirements, even late in development. Agile processes harness change for the customer's competitive advantage.

- Our highest priority is to satisfy the customer through early and continuous delivery of valuable software.

The business challenge is understood by all, and agility is being used to solve the business challenge ahead. By doing so, you're moving the needle more and more to the left side of the Agile values statement. You don't need business executives to become experts in Agile. That is what agile coaches are for.

In the next section is a technique that has helped me for many years when performing an Agile team and organizational health check.

Spider Diagram

The Agile Manifesto gives a 360-degree view instead of looking at an isolated business goal. Whenever I work with clients through an Agile health check, a spider diagram like the one in Figure 4.3 has always been a convincing tool to identify the current condition. It can also provide insights in determining the next target condition. That applies to teams or organizations.

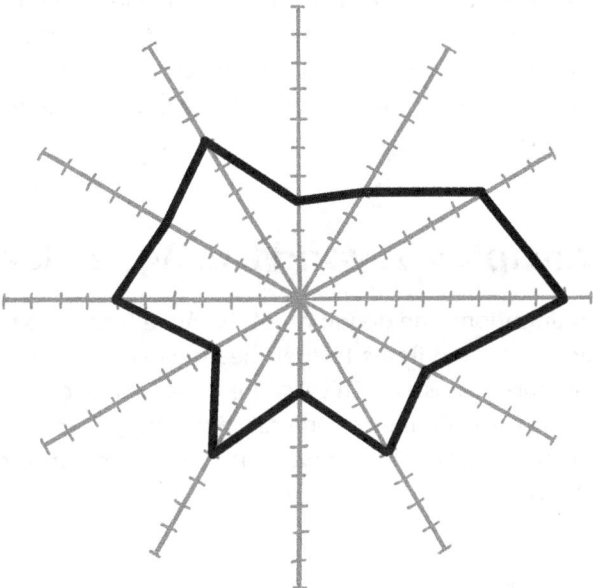

Figure 4.3
Spider diagram (also known as a radar chart)

It is very common that Agile coaches have their personal favorite among the 12 principles. Let's pick "Welcome changing requirements, even late in development. Agile processes harness change for the customer's competitive advantage." Combine that with a passion for teaching, and you might soon find yourself in a training room teaching courses about user stories or product backlog management.

Of course, there's always room for improvement, including backlog management, but it might not be the highest priority. Creating a spider diagram can help shed light on areas that have been neglected and need to come back into focus.

This spider diagram, also referred to as a "radar chart," has the advantage that it can make the current state of agility visually transparent. It provides a view of agility back to the team, coaches, and leaders. That assumes, of course, that stakeholders, customers, and the team are part of the group creating the spider diagram. This is a team effort—not somebody assessing someone else.

If you're in a supporting role, I suggest distancing yourself entirely from that process and taking the role of a facilitator. I also suggest calling it a health check rather than an assessment because it's similar to a medical health check that's done on a regular basis. Those health checks are typically a bit more spaced out and serve more as a trend rather than as a precise tool.

It's easy to go overboard with this approach and craft a complicated, time-consuming activity, which is opposite of the intent here. Maybe it's appropriate to do it every two or three months—a quarterly rhythm might be a good starting point. But always keep in mind who your audience is: the team and those outside supporting the team. It serves as a tool to reflect the progress you're making about increasing agility, and not as a tool to measure performance or productivity. Review the tool with everyone and make changes as needed. If you hear that the cadence is too frequent, slow down. When you reflect too infrequently, or if the tool itself needs to be adjusted, go ahead and make these changes. Always let common sense guide you. Should you hear that the health check is not effective, try something else. One alternative is the traffic light tool explained later in this chapter.

Values and Principles Beyond the Agile Manifesto

For some teams and organizations, the definition of the Agile Manifesto from 2001 does not go far enough. They would like to add items to their health check that connects their team with their unique company culture or mission. This is a great idea, as long as any of these additional items do not contradict the Agile Manifesto. One silly example, just to make a point here, is that introducing micromanagement would not go well with your Agile transformation and would be one of those contradictions.

Many leaders are striving to enable a learning culture within their organization, not only as a way to learn as a team but also as an individual. As humans, we are curious by nature, and we like to learn new things.

Not only do we typically leave work more positive if we have learned something new that day, but it also benefits the company. Just picture a situation where someone had hired a software engineer who is an expert in a specific programming language, but as history repeats itself, that programming language may become less relevant over time. Embracing an active learning culture could not only keep the employee up to date with industry trends but also reduce your pain points in locating talent down the road that possesses those skills. It is clearly a win-win situation.

Besides a learning culture, additional criteria could also include

- Support

- Autonomy

- Mission

- Process

Sometimes, I see teams include "fun" as a criterion to their self-assessment. As much as I hope everybody on a team will be having fun at work, I would not include a criterion like that in an assessment. Lyssa Adkins[6] refers to Agile teams as "high-performing teams," which I like as well. Through becoming more agile, Agile coaches develop their high-performing teaming skills. Agile coaches help the teams become high-performing by using agility. Fun will emerge as a result of working in Agile ways effectively, but fun is not the reason people come to work. Check with your team to find out how they feel about it. In either case, if you are adding your own criteria to your health check, make sure everybody has a clear understanding of what it means and whether there is something they should be aware of when rating themselves.

Traffic Light Indicator

Instead of a 1 to 10 scale, or whatever range you prefer, you can also use a table with traffic light indicators, as shown in Figure 4.4. Green (or medium gray in a black-and-white illustration) represents all good, yellow (light gray) means problems, and red (black) indicates bad. The traffic light indicator is something that served me well when using it with some of my clients over the years.

---

6.   Lyssa Adkins, *Coaching Agile Teams*, Addison-Wesley, 2010.

In addition to the color of a traffic light, an arrow up or down can give additional insights for everybody supporting the team. No arrow at all means stagnant. Each column represents a team, and each row a specific success criterion such as each of the Agile principles.

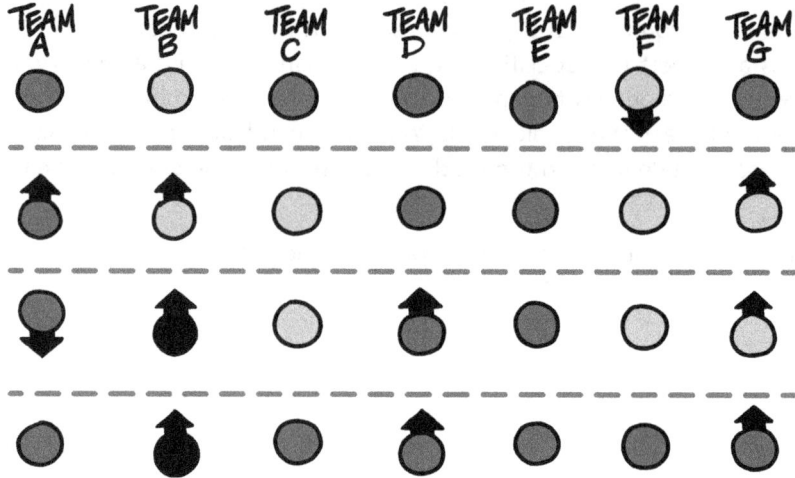

Figure 4.4
Indicators with trend arrows

The color and trend combination provides great additional insight. At first you might have a positive association with Team C or Team E, but both teams are stagnant. There is no trend line up or down. Those teams might not be experimenting with their ways of working or not have the time for experimenting. These insights could be a great starting point for coaching. On the other hand, Team A is all green and is very transparent with trend lines going in different directions. I would interpret this as a higher level of trust and transparency. Team B, as alarming as the red might first appear, is actually working on improvements, is transparent, and believes that the current experiments are perceived as positive. The same is true for Team G.

Give your health check your own flavor by adding additional criteria that are specific to your company's mission and philosophy and linking results to the current condition. We also found great success creating extra space on the storyboard to track the connections between the principles and values and the next target condition, as shown in Figure 4.5.

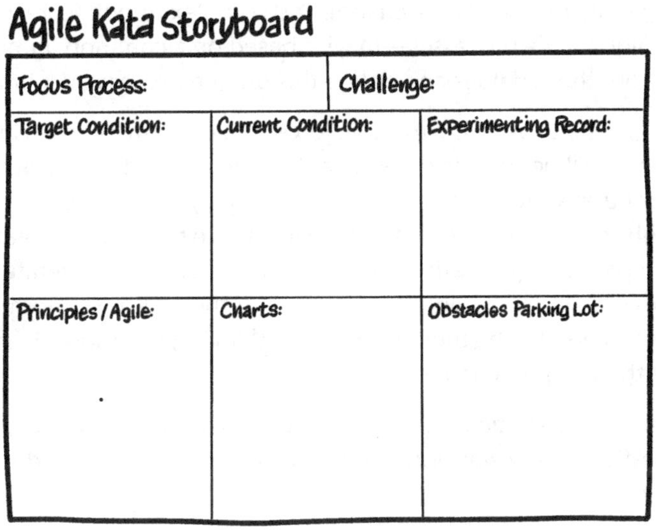

Agile Kata Storyboard

Focus Process:		Challenge:	
Target Condition:	Current Condition:	Experimenting Record:	
Principles / Agile:	Charts:	Obstacles Parking Lot:	

Figure 4.5
Agile Kata storyboard (Adapted from Learner Storyboard in The Toyota Kata Practice Guide *(2018) by Mike Rother.)*

Conclusions: Connecting the Agile Manifesto and Agile Kata

In a 2022 Agile business report published in association with the Agile Alliance,[7] 76 percent of the responders said they failed to achieve their goals in their Agile transformation, and 48 percent of the respondents provided "lack of cultural change" as their number one challenge.

We can certainly argue that the goals of the Agile transformation may not have been adequate in the first place. That does not change the fact that the expectations are poorly managed when transitioning to Agile ways of working. A definition of Agile and a system to assess the current health of agility are therefore critically important. How else could we otherwise later look back from time to time to see if we are going in the right direction and reaching our goals?

The 2022 report also reveals that using Agile techniques and tools are equally important because they foster an Agile culture while a team or organization is transforming. An Agile culture is not the result of a transformation; the culture changes through habit changes, one at time, over time.

In the coming years, the desire for agility is likely to continue to increase. Even if the name is something different than Agile down the road, I can't imagine that the business world will be about less experimentation, unstable requirements, and infrequent improvement. Businesses

---

7.   https://www.agilealliance.org/agile-business-special-report-in-the-times/

are constantly facing an increasing rate of change and complexity, not decreasing. What I can see is a trend to more unique Agile processes—maybe based on a common framework, maybe not. Agile Kata can bring out these details and define this unique process over time.

At the time of writing, generative AI is a massive force that puts stress on existing org-structures. For some, generative AI will be seen as the answer to agility. This idea is to get people out of the way because the computer systems won't create bureaucracy and will deliver agility however we ask them to. Although I'm a big believer in the transformative power of generative AI and believe in its potential to be part of organizational transformation and to accelerate change, I still put people in the driver's seat. I believe with the potential of the real-time information and insights from AI, we humans will need to be more thoughtful, thinking in a more clear-headed scientific way, as we navigate the wings of change.

I believe the meta skill of scientific thinking with goals, hypotheses, and experimentations are here to stay. The question is how well and rapidly we will learn it and how determined we are to continuously improve.

If you go back to the definition of the Improvement Kata pattern in Part I, it says nothing about finding best Agile practices and implementing them. In fact, the implementation mindset, where you try to copy someone else's best practices or implement a specific set of tools, is decidedly unscientific.

Instead, it asks you to develop a vision for what you need to be in the future, like the Agile Manifesto, then back up from there and ask what big challenges you want to overcome. Then you work to get there by experimenting and learning. We are truly finding our way, not assuming we have the independent variables up front to control our way to defined outcomes.

Reflection

- How do you personally react to change?
- How are you judged in your organization for success?
- What does Agile mean in your team or organization?
- Which Agile principles are your company's most and least favorite?
- How do you embody an Agile mindset in your organization?
- How do you grow agility in your organization?
- What parameters in your organization tell you that you are improving agility?

5

Measuring Value

Ask anyone who knows Agile what it is about, and they are sure to mention customer and value. Products and services must add value to the customer.

But what is value? It is a somewhat amorphous term. Organizations and teams can focus all their energy on creating value for their clients, but at the end, it is the recipient who decides whether it's valuable to them. Value is not necessarily equivalent with the highest-quality solution, as the battle of video systems between Video 2000 and VHS in the 1980s demonstrated.

I think the customer wants at least the following four things from software:

1. **It works.** It solves the specific problem intended.

2. **It's user friendly.** They do not need to wade through long user manuals or call a help desk, and the features most important to them appear almost seamlessly.

3. **It works every time.** It is reliable, does not crash, and delivers consistent, accurate results.

4. **It's cost effective.** The value is what they get relative to what they have to pay.

This suggests a series of measurements from the final product and service the customer experiences (Figure 5.1), working back to the process that produces the product and service.

Figure 5.1
Effective development

The customer doesn't care what the development process looks like, but the organization producing the software must if they want to consistently produce what the customer wants, when they want it, at a competitive price point, and make money doing it.

Let's assume you have measures of the process, resulting software, and customer satisfaction. What is the purpose of these measures? Consider the following two reasons:

- **External control:** Management is running the business and wants to make money and be competitive in the marketplace. They often have a need to feel that they are in control. One of the uses of a dashboard of key performance indicators (KPIs) is to hand over control to management. Like driving a car, you cannot run the company without having reliable metrics that show how well the system is operating so you can make appropriate adjustments.

- **Internal performance and learning:** Those who are doing the work need data so they can know how they are doing and identify any deviations from the standard. What should be happening? What is happening? What are the gaps you need to close to achieve what you want? What can you learn from each step that will help make the next step better? This is measurement to help successful delivery of the product-service, make course corrections, and learn and improve.

First, I explore those two views a bit more, and then I share concrete examples of how value can be measured.

Metrics for Management

In traditional ways of working, we believe that it is critical that we identify the precise correct measures and hold people accountable to them. Senior executives are most likely to try to manage via the numbers that affect the outcomes they desire, like sales, costs, and EBITDA (earnings before interest, taxes, depreciation, and amortization). Middle managers are being pressured for operational outcomes like productivity, on-time delivery, and customer satisfaction. Agile teams are often focused on products; if they meet a schedule, things are fine, but when things go wrong they are unduly pressured. This often leads to many pressure points and a political game where numbers are massaged over time such that actual transparency is compromised.

Management needs metrics to manage against. However, there is a risk in traditional management of managers trying to exert too much control. The reality is that there are limits to management control regardless of how many things are measured and how well they're measured. Management is not actually doing the work of providing customer value, but they're trying to influence those who do the work to create value. The types of general metrics they're seeing on the dashboard give them general indications that some things are going right and others are going wrong, but they do not have the fidelity to know exactly what is happening. That insight is only gained visiting the place where the work is happening—the gemba. Otherwise, they are likely to jump to broad conclusions and take broad actions that may hurt more than help, or at least be a waste of time and money. In other words, they often think in business terms about the results they want and take actions that are decidedly unscientific.

Improvement Kata starts with a broad challenge, which may be something like "reliable, accurate, user-friendly tax package delivered in half the time and half the cost of competitive software." What you need to measure is the final outcome: what the customer experiences, characteristics of the software (like reliability), and characteristics of the process (such as lead time).

The point of the target conditions is to provide measurable goals of the software and process on the way to the big challenge. Improvement Kata focuses on the process of creating value for the customer scientifically.

For dashboards used for extrinsic control, it's important to use the critical few metrics you will standardize on to make it easy for the managers to check the temperature of the people and process. Here, kata can help leaders focusing on a process to weed through a dashboard and isolate a few metrics that are valuable for management but are also measuring value.

There certainly is value in a few standard metrics and management dashboards to check the general temperature of the business, but for the process of improving scientifically, you focus on metrics that are useful for the teams to create value for customers.

Metrics for Teams

The developers who create the product need the measures to set goals and check on how they are doing relative to those goals. The challenge needs to be measurable, as do the target conditions. Gaps between desired and actual tell them where they need to put their effort and help them to learn to get better in the future. The measures are intrinsic to the value-added process.

For improvement, a particular team can use the common KPIs, but when they define a target condition or obstacle, they may need to invent a specific metric, use it to accomplish their goals, and then throw it away. It is not a concern that they will confuse the management system with too many metrics. This approach is drastically different when Agile teams use metrics today. It is still very common in organizations not only to strive for a static set of metrics across the entire development cycle but also to standardize across all teams. A metric, which might have a lifespan only to the next target condition, can provide additional opportunities to reflect on an experiment.

In Agile, we learn that the customer is first, so we want customer-focused metrics. We also learn that we should deliver software frequently, and working software is the primary measure of progress, so we need metrics that reflect the customer quality and reliability of small software features in real time. We want this process to be efficient, maximizing the amount of software done in a period of time, so we need to measure this progress, and related cost, as we do development. From the point of view of the actual creation of the software, managers looking at and reacting to software can easily become part of the bureaucracy. With Agile, the hope is to keep bureaucracy to a minimum.

There is a different way of thinking about measures. First, there has been a more holistic view of measures beyond business outcomes. Second, there has been much debate about operational outcomes. The Agile community has managed to move beyond velocity and gotten more subtle with measures like number of increments (not releases!), quality (code coverage, for example), number of impediments resolved, and value produced (number of subscribers, customers, new products launches, and so on).

When you get to the teams of those who create the product, the use of metrics is often different and not necessarily linked to the metrics used by executives—for example, unit tests that can help the developers check whether the code works as expected. There are certainly acceptance criteria, nonfunctional requirements, and a definition of done, all of which can help measure success.

And there are also traditional measures, like cost and schedule. The problem with those measures is that teams have little to no control over them, and most of the time, the team was not involved in the decision-making process in the first place. Many developers do not have a lot of tools to measure how they are doing the work and how they can improve the work. Let's explore next how this issue can be tackled.

Value

Have you ever been in or observed a situation where a customer was very vocal about something that took way too long, and the teams working on it felt like a well-oiled Agile machine? This is quite common and relates to the difference between cycle time and lead time, as shown in Figure 5.2.

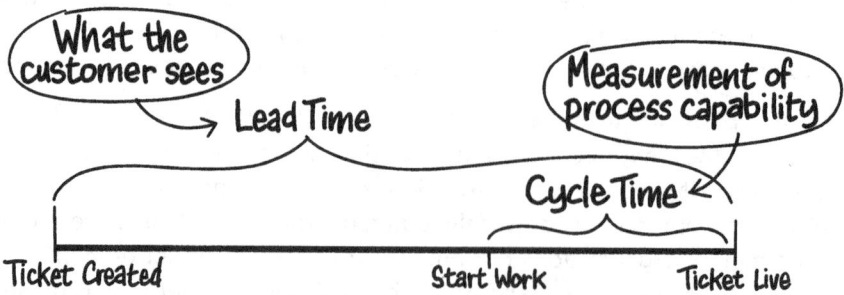

Figure 5.2
Lead and cycle time

The clock for cycle time begins ticking when the team picks up a ticket (for example, a user story or feature request) and ends when the user story is completed. Cycle time is often based on a previously agreed-on definition of done (DoD) and acceptance criteria. If a team can do something like this in a very short period, the perception is that work was turned around quickly. If the customer submitted that feature request many weeks or months earlier, they will perceive the process overall as a slow turnaround. If cycle time is very slow, lead time is never fast. But fast cycle time alone does not result in a fast lead time, which can lead to the misconceptions between a customer and a team's perception of their capability.

Cycle time is an important indication for an Agile team to know how fast and efficiently they work as a team. It is important because that is typically the area a team has control over.

Just jumping to the next request and finishing it as quickly as possible to keep cycle time low is not ideal either. There can be very good reasons for a team to delay work on a certain feature because not every newly identified feature is automatically important. Triaging requests by categories into different buckets becomes important, and deleting the feature requests that aren't important or the ones that don't fit into the product strategy is a key activity when triaging. Just because somebody thought about a feature and wrote it down does not mean that it needs to be implemented. Simplicity, the art of maximizing the work not done, is essential. This not only is a good mantra in general but also represents one of the 12 principles of the Agile Manifesto.

However, there are situations where the overall response time is important and lead time, the time from request to delivery, is key. The effectiveness of an Agile organization is the ability to react to changing market environments and to produce value. That translates directly into a timeline from recognizing the change or a new feature to releasing it, which is lead time. Doing this in an efficient way helps, but being effective is so much more important. Following is a quick example.

Manual Versus Automated Solutions

I worked with a company that quickly shifted gears in the late 1990s during the early days of the dot-com bubble. They decided to offer online products with an annual subscription plan. The online product itself was a simple consumer product, easy to understand, just like buying cloud storage today. As a consumer, you're just buying terabytes of storage. Behind the scenes, hidden to the consumer, there are many complexities and business rules that aren't visible to you.

Many of this company's competitors, part of the gold rush, decided to build a technical solution to deal with those complexities and went to the drawing board. Because Agile processes were not well known back then, many of these companies began with requirements sessions, followed by analysis and design, leading to a waterfall process. The company I worked with did something drastically different.

They decided to create a simple website that had an input field and an Order Now button next to it. When someone ordered the product, an email was sent to a call center that processed the order manually by phone. Yes, by phone! The customer had no idea that their click would trigger a manual process in the background. The perception of the customers was indeed the opposite. The brand was perceived as fast, innovative, and, most important, delivering value. Obviously, this was an inefficient and costly way of fulfilling an order, but because the online products were in high in demand, customers came in droves as they decided to favor slow over not-at-all. The competitive edge was truly in favor of the manual solution. Of course, lead time was much slower than any fully automated solution, but their competition was far away from fulfilling any orders at all.

The key phrase in this business model was *annual subscription*. The bigger the first initial wave of customers, the higher the chances of receiving renewals the following year. So, this quick and simple approach to take orders was not giving them a one-time competitive advantage. The advantage would repeat every year. And while they were cranking up their customer base early, they began building a fully automated solution in parallel. They had early revenue, important insights in a new business domain, and a large customer base for renewals their competitors could only dream of. And yes, much of the most amazing software from their competition never saw the light of day.

The challenge in Agile Kata describes a problem, not a solution. A self-organized group of business and engineering staff, using a commonsense approach, can go a long way. If a target condition is defined as taking an online product order and the achieve-by date is near, a group is almost forced into out-of-the-box thinking. Of course, that doesn't mean that a group would come up with low-quality solutions, but it allows for additional viewpoints that would otherwise be ignored.

If the refined challenge includes fast, reliable, and cost-effective processing of orders down the road, an automated solution is inevitable.

Types of Value

How do you define and measure value in your organization? Are you a for-profit or not-for-profit business domain? Are you measuring the number of new products you've launched this year, or are you solely improving an existing product? Are you interested in the ratio between revenue and number of employees or the revenue growth in general? After a few years of revenue growth, maybe profit margins gain importance, especially if you have shareholders. How is your customer satisfaction or retention rate? Do organizations in the not-for-profit domain measure success rates of their programs, long-term sustainability, and impact of a program? These are a few examples companies can provide as an orientation for decision-making.

In the early 2000s, LEGO realized that too much diversification and products alien to the original product line had a negative impact on the brand, customers, and profit. A company-wide refocus on the original product line turned the ship around for the toy maker.[1] LEGO has a strong lean culture,[2] uses Kata, and has a learning culture that is built on experimenting.

Because Agile organizations are focused on delivering early and continuous value, any measurements taken while performing Agile Kata should be connected to a metric that is important for your longer-term strategy.

If you're using Agile Kata to replace existing Agile processes like Scrum, measuring value on a team level becomes very important as well. Measuring velocity, user story points, or hours "burned" in a so-called burn-down chart are ineffective. Unfortunately, so many Agile teams do these things. Measuring the number of increments per sprint or measuring quality are much more powerful. (Read more about Agile Kata as a team process in the use cases in Part III.)

In one of my podcast episodes, Luke Hohmann[3] shared a story about an Agile team that focused on one measurement only: the number of defects found in production. Think about it: Fewer defects found in production means fewer costs for customer care. It also means more satisfied customers, increased developer morale, more time for building new features instead of fixing defects, and, of course, a healthier product base to integrate future feature requests.

As part of setting up Agile Kata in your organization, identifying and agreeing on what "value" is becomes a critical exercise. Keep in mind that organizations typically strive for achieving more than one goal—for example, a mix of profitability, quality, and maybe even some sort of philanthropy. As you can see, some goals are contradictory, so the goal is a healthy balance between them. Think of speed of delivery and quality. Those have to be evaluated and balanced based on the domain you are in. Teams building games played on a phone versus teams building systems for medical devices require a different balanced approach. The diversity of business domains and company cultures makes it impossible to provide any cookie cutter recommendations.

Still, there are two metrics that I recommend evaluating for any strategy: lead time combined with a product-quality metric like number of increments or number of defects found in production. The number of increments tells you how many times a team was able to create a potentially shippable product. Without good quality and a functioning architecture, the number of increments would be most likely low. These are metrics that have served me very well because they look at value and quality at the same time.

When you begin measuring lead time, I am almost certain that you will notice a big issue sooner or later. It's called wait time. The longer your lead time is in comparison to the cycle time, the more wait time is part of your process. That means, whatever the reason for your wait time is, it impacts your customers negatively because they are getting the anticipated features slower than needed. And that is not because of skills and capabilities. It is the time when partially done

1.   https://www.theceomagazine.com/business/company-profile/rebuilding-lego/

2.   https://www.lego.com/en-us/aboutus/lego-group/the-lego-brand?locale=en-us

3.   https://www.agile.fm/agilefm/luke-hohmann

work sits idly as it waits to be finished. Congratulations, you just found a starting point for continuous improvement!

To help you get started, you could incorporate a Wait column following any columns on your Kanban or Scrum board. If you transition work from one team or department to another, those teams also need wait columns. A tool that automates time-tracking based on time spent in each state is mandatory, in my opinion. Doing this by hand is certainly not realistic.

What does the Wait column do for you? It separates the value-added time from the non-value-added time. During wait time, no value is being added to the product or service. Wait time is not the only non-value time, but in IT, it plays a more important factor compared to production and manufacturing where transportation or inventory, for example, can be very important factors, too.

Dividing the total value-added time by the total lead time and multiplying that by 100 gives you an important metric called Process Cycle Efficiency (PCE).[4] A high PCE indicates that a team is spending a big portion of their time on adding value.

Nigel Thurlow, who wrote the foreword to this book, also provided a small case study of this approach being used by a global telecoms company he coached and helped to implement this approach. Jira was the tool used to track work. The first step was to map the end-to-end process flow for work that was being done. Each processing step, such as development, testing, integration, and so on was identified, and a column was created for each of them. Preceding each column, an additional queueing column or waiting column was added.

As work progressed and exited, a processing step would enter the queue for the next process. As Jira "cards" were moved by the team to the next state, Jira would record the date and time automatically. As work progressed, the lead time between processes that included both the time processing (when work was happening) plus the wait time for each next step was recorded. The results were then exported from Jira and imported into Power BI because the latter has better visualization capabilities.

Once the data was in Power BI, the calculations of PCE for the overall lead time (also called time to market) could be calculated, as well as the PCE for each step in the work lifecycle. This then provides the opportunity for improvement activity that Agile Kata is designed to support. It also provides leadership and management with valuable insights into where constraints exist in the workflow and enables discussions around resourcing the system and workload balancing.

If you don't want to build your own dashboard and metric system from scratch, in the next sections, I talk about two popular approaches among Agile professionals that can help you get started: evidence-based management and objectives and key results. Please keep in mind that tools and frameworks are just starting points that then need to be improved and refined over time.

---

4.   https://nigelthurlow.com/all-about-lean-metrics/

Evidence-Based Management

It's hard to imagine, but when seat belts were first introduced in automobiles in the 1970s, they weren't mandatory. New York became the first state in the United States that made wearing a seat belt law in 1984. Eleven years later, all states except New Hampshire had made it a legal requirement. Plenty of evidence exists to support that it was a good idea to make it a legal requirement that people wear a seat belt. In 2017, according to the National Highway Traffic Safety Administration, 15,000 lives were saved in the United States alone by "clicking it." The WHO reports a similar conclusion in a global study. It states that in countries where the seat belt law is strictly enforced, fatalities are lower than in countries that are lax about the law.

Even though the seat belt law was heavily debated in the 1970s, the evidence that it saves more lives than causes death, which it rarely does, became clearly evident.

The core idea of evidence-based management (EBM[5]) is to reduce bias and intuition but also ignore personal experience when it comes to decision-making. For example, I might have a personal connection to a car accident in which somebody was hurt from a seat belt, but that does not change the fact that many more people benefit or survive because of wearing one.

EBM had its origin in the fields of medicine and education in the 1990s, where it supports empirical decision-making based on scientific evidence. The approach started being used in the business world in the 2000s to help leaders and managers make decisions based on facts and key metrics.

I have seen so many organizations start their Agile journey with a specific Agile process. It doesn't matter which one. When executives are asked some years later if the transformation led to the desired results, many of them struggle to provide concrete answers. Of course, they often have a gut feeling and feedback that things have improved, but did the situation actually improve? And by how much? How can you make sure that the investment into an Agile transformation was a good idea? Many leaders and Agile coaches struggle to produce an answer to that question.

One of the many reasons why so many organizations cannot produce that evidence is that many do not take baseline measurements of the current condition before they begin their journeys. Instead of taking the time to step back to identify the key metrics that are supporting the case of Agile processes, many jump right in. Any assessment might bring topics to the surface that are the reasons why leaders are looking at Agile processes. The four key values of EBM are time to market, ability to innovate, current value, and unrealized value (Figure 5.3). The next sections look at each one.

---

5.   Sometimes also abbreviated as *EbMgt*.

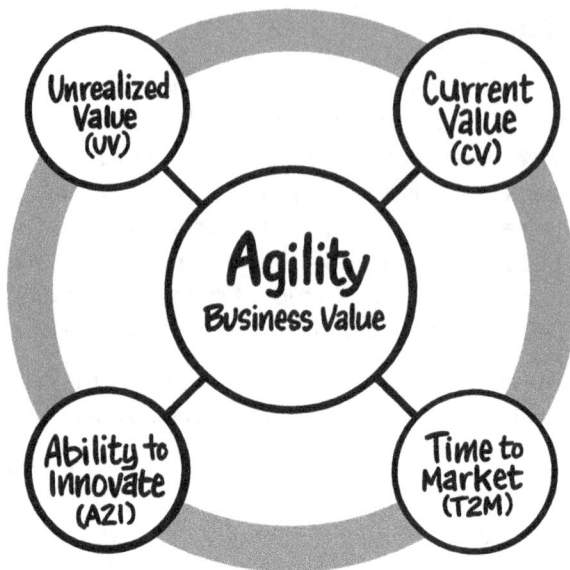

Figure 5.3
Evidence-based management[6] (Adapted from Scrum.org, https://www.scrum.org/resources/evidence-based-management.)

Time to Market (T2M)

How long does it take for a company to launch a new product or revise it? If your competition is much better at the game, transitioning to Agile processes to reduce T2M could be one great cornerstone for your transformation. What is known as T2M in EBM is the same as lead time.[7] When many departments or teams are part of going live, you might break the goals down to the team level. For example, an Agile team that is not completing a product from start to finish can focus on increasing the number of increments per iteration. Even though that does not reduce T2M on its own, it's an important stepping stone. Each increment represents a potentially shippable sliver of your product. The more increments you produce, the more you could potentially ship.

Increments are therefore a positive enabler for the overarching business goal, while giving the team a subgoal they can reach by themselves.

Ability to Innovate (A2I)

If your code quality is low and therefore hard to maintain, chances are small that a team can easily integrate an amazing new feature the product managers are thinking of into the existing code

---

6. [KMBR2024]

7. https://nigelthurlow.com/all-about-lean-metrics/

base. Or worse, you won't be able to integrate it at all. I've seen code where everyone around me warned me, "Don't touch this!" The code is working, but everyone is afraid to revise it because the side effects are not fully understood.

In situations like this, the "ability to innovate" is expensive, slow, and sometimes not possible at all. An ability to innovate is given if the code quality and architectural standards are high. Unit testing, regression testing, and test automation are critical factors for that. Every line of code written needs to be tested over and over again and would repeat for each increment several times. The effort therefore grows exponentially. This approach also sheds light on the step of writing the line of code in the first place. Is that part of an important feature or a nice to have? Are there ways this should be expressed more elegantly or be refactored?

Being able to innovate is a key criterion in striving for business agility. I have used examples from software engineering; I'm sure you can make a connection from this field to your domain if you are in another industry. A2I connects directly to one of the 12 principles of the Agile Manifesto: "Continuous attention to technical excellence and good design enhances agility."

Value (Current and Unrealized)

Equipped with a metric that gives us evidence that we are lowering the time-to-market and a metric that tells us that we are able to innovate, EBM also measures two forms of values: the current value and the unrealized (potential) value.

Net promoter score, customer satisfaction score, revenue growth rate, and revenue per employee are just a few examples of current value. Those criteria are dependent on the type of business and the goals you're pursuing.

Identifying the market share gap can help to gauge the untapped potential (unrealized value) of a company entering or impacting that market growth segment. Netflix explored unrealized value when they transitioned from a technical streaming platform to also being a production company of shows and content. Spotify tapped into the podcast market and began producing shows. These are just two somewhat recent examples of companies identifying unrealized value potential.

Applying EBM with Agile Kata

None of these value areas of EBM will change overnight by introducing EBM or Agile Kata. That would be a false expectation. There is a reason why the key value areas start with the word *key*. They represent your overall agile strategy. I suggest starting with one metric for each key value area and frequently review and adjust as needed. Dashboards with too much information can overload and easily distract people.

EBM and Agile Kata make great companions. The four key value areas can give an organization a strategic direction and focus. These value areas can then influence and trickle down to teams performing Agile Kata and turn more into actionable steps. On the flip side, the results and find-ings by applying Agile Kata can then lay the foundation to adjust the key value areas of your EBM setup. Those ideas are intertwined.

EBM and Agile Kata can have great synergy, and Agile Kata can make EBM an even more robust framework for achieving organizational excellence. For example, each key value area can help determine whether directions or target conditions have been reached. Experimentation records created during Agile Kata can produce important evidence of the gained efficiency or effective-ness. The records can be a powerful tool for future strategic adjustments.

The rise of generative AI can be an even bigger opportunity to analyze experimentation records and internal documentation. As Agile Kata spreads within an organization into different func-tions, one overall strategy can keep all Agile Kata focused on organizational goals and objectives.

Objectives and Key Results

The objectives and key results (OKR) framework is another popular tool for goal setting in orga-nizations and has resonated well with Agile professionals in recent years. OKRs are not new. Andy Grove[8] created OKRs in the 1970s at Intel, but they didn't become popular until they were introduced at Google in the early 2000s.[9]

OKR is similar to EBM in that there are two connections between OKRs and Agile Kata worth exploring:

- Applying scientific thinking to implement the desired objectives within an organization

- Using scientific thinking to introduce OKRs into an organization

OKRs are a structured way to set and communicate strategic objectives. On the other hand, Agile Kata is a disciplined approach to continuously improve and achieve these objectives. In the OKR framework, objectives are broken down into smaller results, and Agile Kata and a series of target conditions bring you closer to the goal. Objectives are clear and prioritized, while Agile Kata uses an inspect-and-adapt approach that helps teams navigate to the goals over time.

Some objectives are visionary and strategic. As much as this is a positive thing, they would be too far out for using 1:1 as a challenge in Agile Kata. Breaking those long-term objectives down into three- to six-month objectives can provide a clear challenge in Agile Kata (step 1).

On a shorter time scale, key results can provide a great starting point for Agile Kata teams defin-ing their next target condition.

---

8.   https://en.wikipedia.org/wiki/Objectives_and_key_results

9.   [JD2018]

Although OKR cycles and Agile Kata are independent from each other, they can work well with each other. Agile Kata can bring a continuous improvement and pattern to the many organizations that are using the OKR framework and looking for a way to implement their objectives. OKRs can also provide a structure between short-term tactical results and long-term strategic goals by translating them to challenges and target conditions.

Typical challenges when introducing OKRs in an organization are

- Goals that are too aggressive

- Lack of review cycles

- Culture that resists change[10]

Of course, nobody is safe from picking goals that are too aggressive, and that includes Agile Kata practitioners. But practicing scientific thinking forces a critical evaluation of the objectives on a regular basis. The gap between current condition and target condition should be narrow. Experiments to close that gap are executed by a series of PDCA cycles that are very frequent—at times, more than once a day. Deliberate practice is an integral part of the Kata mindset, and changing habits into new norms is key to transforming a culture that resists change.

You will see more concrete ideas for using Agile Kata in Part III, but if you're evaluating whether to introduce OKRs into your organization, Agile Kata could be your partner. Instead of a big-bang implementation approach across an entire organization, start small, do baby steps, learn, and evolve.

Reflection

- How quickly can you adapt to changes in requirements and market conditions, and what processes do you have in place to facilitate this?

- Evaluate your emphasis on customer collaboration.

- How do you ensure continuous improvement in your processes, practices, and products?

- How transparent are you with progress and challenges, both internally and with your customers?

- What measures do you use to assess agility?

- How often do you review and adjust these measures so they stay relevant?

- What is your balance between creating valuable outcomes versus producing internal documentation?

---

10.   [JD2018]

6

Agile Coaching

I bet at some point in your life, you had help learning a difficult skill, whether it was in sports, music, cooking, a new language, or myriad other skills. In sports, we call these teachers coaches, but they all have common characteristics. They break down the skill into micro-skills and ask us to practice repeatedly until we've achieved mastery. Then we move on to practicing further skills and eventually put these skills together until we can complete a difficult task, play a challenging piece of music, or make a complete meal. Some endeavors are individual, like singles tennis, and others are team sports like football, which requires both individual practice and group practice. It's possible to do it yourself and learn from a book or computer program, but we tend to learn better and faster with a coach.

Throughout one's life, teachers take different forms (educator, facilitator, trainer) to scaffold and guide new knowledge (chemistry, management, mathematics) or skills (communication, leadership, management). Regardless of the context, coaches, teachers, and facilitators share some common characteristics. Each has the expertise to break down a skill into micro-skills so that they're easier to learn and, eventually, be mastered. Achieving a master-level rank for a particular skill is indicative of one who can apply that skill in the real world, showing pragmatic utility. Skills can be individual skills or team skills.

Effective coaches open a new perspective for the coachee to help them find a path through the unknown. This is often accomplished when the coach asks powerful questions or challenges the coachee to accomplish something beyond their current capability. A coach can walk the walk and has the social skills to maintain a healthy relationship.

The role of an Agile coach has a long tradition. In addition to 1:1 professional coaching to develop an individual's skills, an Agile coach is typically working with teams and navigating the synergy of the highly skilled professionals in those teams. The various tools and methods of Agile provide a structure for the coach to develop people and teamwork.

Consider these questions about coaching in Agile Kata:

- Are there any changes to the role of an Agile coach when teams work scientifically?
- How can Agile coaches serve teams through the steps of goal setting and experimenting in a self-organized way?
- Can the structure of Improvement Kata aid Agile coaches in developing important skills and ways of working that enhance goal achievement and teamwork?

This chapter looks at the discipline of coaching in general and reflects on the stances of an Agile coach. It concludes with the impact Agile Kata has on the role of Agile coaches.

Coaching Outside of Business

I can't tell you any professional sport where a team or individual does not work with a coach. Even the best athletes have coaches. Consider elite golfers and their personal coaches. In the rare event that a team is without a coach, it is most likely because of a temporary unplanned situation.

Interestingly, in the context of professional sports, the coach has often played at a much lower level than the players they might be coaching. You might wonder what a number one tennis player can learn from a coach who has never played on the same level as the coachee.

We are used to the picture of a coach in the audience of a tennis tournament or a coach on the sidelines of a team sport like football, soccer, or baseball. What we do not see are the many hours of practice that preceded those events. The coach may not be able to demonstrate the skills they are teaching at the level of their best students, but they can see good and bad form, have the instincts to assign the correct drills at the right time, and are effective in communicating weaknesses and countermeasures. They give us better feedback on our strengths and weaknesses than we can give ourselves, and they help motivate us to get better.

Surprisingly, knowing of the power of coaching, we're not used to the role of coaches in the business world—at least not as formalized or publicly visible. Many successful people can point to an informal mentor who made a huge difference in their careers, yet few of us at work have benefited from a formal system of coaching nearly as sophisticated as in professional sports. The International Coaching Federation (ICF) issued a report[1] that identifies coaching deficits in business, particularly at the execution level. Coaching can help us learn in new ways, and coaching

---

1. ICF Global Coaching Study 2023

can generate curiosity. A coach can help us reflect. We can then see things we would otherwise not see. Linda Rising, Lifetime Achievement Award winner of the World Agility Forum, sums up nicely what coaches can do so we can see ourselves in a new way:

> We know that children lose some of that curiosity, insight, when they go to school. They pay attention. The best students pay attention. They do what they're told. They get A's on the tests. "I'm not saying they all necessarily become robots, but that's what we're rewarded for—is sitting quietly, paying attention.
>
> Of course, there are always a few. There are some who remain curious, who remain open, who are not afraid to fail, who learn their entire lives. That's really what we want. We want those babies. We want those babies to say, the wonderful scientists that they started out, falling down, it's okay, get up, try again, baby steps. I know, I hope a lot of you haven't forgotten what it's like to be a baby. I hope you're still curious. I hope you're still open. I hope you're still learning. And I'm hoping that Agile Kata will lead the way.[2]

Learning to Learn

There is a dramatic shift of learning and knowledge sharing unfolding in front of us. This can be accelerated through tools like generative artificial intelligence, as well as collaborative technologies like wikis (Hawaiian for *quick*) that enabled crowd-sourced encyclopedias like Wikipedia, which revolutionized and paved the way for dramatic change in learning and knowledge sharing.[3]

As a result, we are seeing the world of work and education change. One milestone is a report released by the U.S. Security of Education with the title "A Nation at Risk"[4] that was released in 1983 to examine the quality of education in the United States. The findings suggested the following twenty-first century desirable skills in the following three categories:

- Learning and innovation skills (critical thinking, problem-solving, collaboration, and creativity)
- Digital literacy skills (information, media, communication)
- Career and life skills (cross-culture, self-direction, initiative, accountability)

One key finding in the report was the recommendation to focus on creating a learning society, which might sound like a lofty goal. But when broken down to companies and organizations, that goal can be much more manageable. For decades, educational institutions have prepared students for the workplace and companies recruited from the talent pool to bring the latest

2. https://www.agilekata.pro/recordings/v/scientific-thinking-and-agile-kata, 21:00

3. WikiWikiWeb was created by Ward Cunningham, one of the 17 signatories of the Agile Manifesto.

4. [US1983]

knowledge in-house. Today, a college degree gives you an entrance into a workplace or field. Once there, you will most likely face a great deal of uncertainty. The skill of *learning how to learn* becomes more and more important for individuals and collectively as a team. Although I find it fascinating that people like Bill Gates, Mark Zuckerberg, and Steve Jobs dropped out of college early and became incredibly successful, there is no evidence that dropping out of college will make anyone similarly successful. However, It does tell us that some creative minds and entrepreneurs had reached their limits with the educational system early and broke off.

So why would we turn off a person's enthusiasm for continuous learning, an interest in work outside their own responsibilities, and a drive to work in teams when they join a company? Instead, a business should be considering how to encourage continuous learning and skill building.

Do your onboarding procedures encourage critical thinking or rote memorization? Do new hires get coaching to practice the types of team skills you expect in your daily work? Are members taught to think scientifically as they work on complex projects to achieve their goals? Are you building a learning organization?

Do you feel that these topics go way beyond agility? Think again! Business agility is the ability to adapt quickly to market changes. How fast an organization can react to customer feedback and pivot effectively in response to new information gained may determine competitiveness.

The Agile Kata can train team members in scientific thinking and help teams to continuously learn through experimentation. Exploration and being able to work in teams is important. Scientific thinking is not only an individual skill, but it also can become an everyday routine for teams. Do teams have the required social skills to work in group settings and collaborate effectively? If not, maybe the Agile coach introduces Agile Kata with a goal to change that. Maybe a kata that focuses on improving team skills?

How do teams craft their process over time by identifying what works for them and what doesn't? Agile Kata enables scientific thinking and working in self-managed teams. It promotes critical thinking by using an evidence-based approach, fitting nicely with what is outlined in the report about twenty-first century skills.

So what does all that have to do with coaching?

If we agree that learning is a lifelong skill and that no university or school can effectively prepare us for all the possibilities that lie ahead of us, then on-the-job training becomes increasingly important.

Of course, off-the-shelf courses and certifications will stay important. So do university degrees and trade schools, but continuous learning can't be the occasional course or refresher based on an annual performance review. In addition to learning in a classroom, the learning needs to turn into actions and be practiced deliberately. Closing the feedback loop with the team about the scientific thinking approach and the reflection on experiments establishes continuous on-the-job learning, improvement, and innovation.

The role of a coach becomes a crucial part of the continuous learning strategy within an organization. The coach can boost and accelerate through new perspectives, reflecting and honing the skills of a learner. Words of encouragement and constructive positive feedback can keep everyone going and create a productive learning environment for all employees.

Therefore, the role of an Agile Kata coach can increase the effectiveness of Agile teams. Agile coaching has been popular for many years, but there is no clear definition and agreed-upon job description for an Agile coach. A common unfortunate misunderstanding is that many believe that Agile coaching is only done by an Agile coach, but it's a skill that isn't a responsibility of only an Agile coach. To be effective, you can utilize Agile coaching frameworks that highlight the important stances that can be the start of a learning journey.

Next, I describe two Agile coaching frameworks that can better help you understand the role of an Agile coach when working with teams applying Agile Kata.

Agile Coaching Competency Frameworks

There are two popular frameworks for agile coaches: the Agile Coaching Competency Framework[5] (Figure 6.1) and the Agile Coaching Growth Wheel[6] (Figure 6.2).

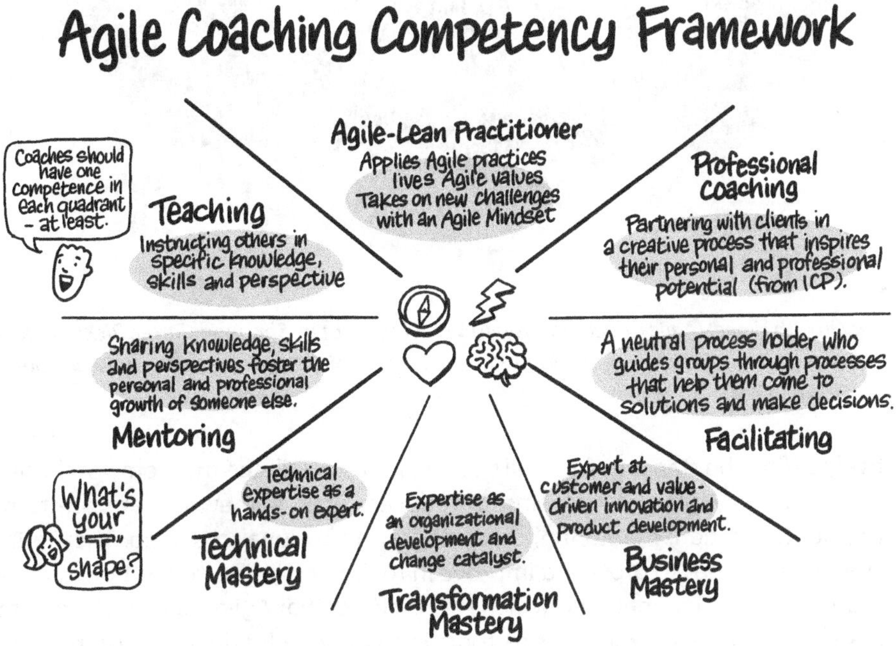

Figure 6.1
Agile Coaching Competency Framework (Adapted from "Agile Coaching Competencies," Lyssa Adkins Blog, Lyssa Adkins and Michael K. Spayd. https://lyssaadkins.com/blog-1/2023/06/22/agile-coaching-competencies/)

---

5. [LA2010]

6. [BG2022]

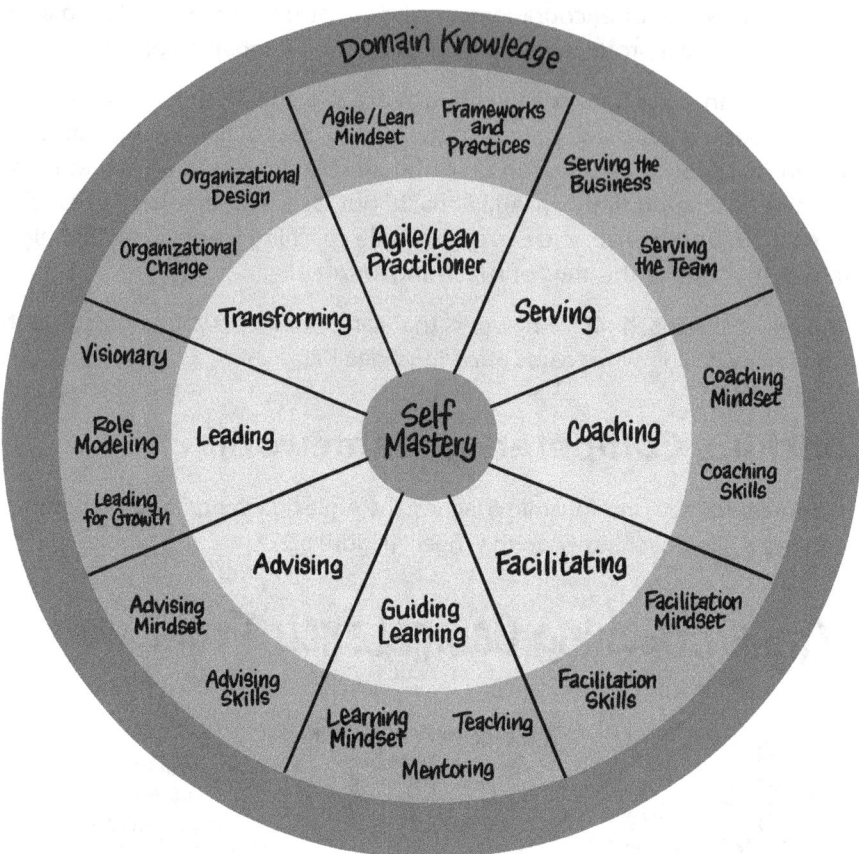

Figure 6.2
Agile Coaching Growth Wheel (Agile Coaching Growth Wheel concept by Shannon Carter, Rickard Jones, Martin Lambert, Stacie Louie, Tom Reynolds, Rohit Ratan, Andre Rubin, Kubair Shirazee, and Mark Summers, licensed under CC BY-SA 4.0.)

Both effectively define the stances of an Agile coach, and you will see that some of these stances will be impacted when Agile Kata is being introduced. Both frameworks are pretty much in agreement about facilitation, mentoring, teaching, or professional coaching. They're intended to be tools for Agile coaches to grow and improve in their roles. Interestingly, both list the Agile-Lean Practitioner as a core competency, which is a reminder that Agile coaches are practitioners, and Agile has its roots in Lean, which has its roots in the Toyota Production System. Hello, Agile Kata!

Agile Coaches can walk the walk in the Agile space and have broad and deep understanding of tools, frameworks, techniques, practices, and values. In the same way you wouldn't ask a tennis instructor to coach you in the sport of golf, the introduction of Agile Kata forces Agile coaches to widen their horizon. This is not just a matter of memorizing the sequence of the Agile Kata pattern, although I believe this is quick, easy, and straightforward. It is more challenging and a very different story to foster a culture of scientific thinking and empiricism within a team. The Agile Kata sequence is the beginning of the scientific thinking journey, not the end.

Both the competency framework and the growth wheel contain a teaching stance that is often misunderstood among Agile coaches. Teaching could be a formal two-day classroom instruction with slides and exercises, but it could also mean short teaching moments that are informal, not in a classroom setting, and maybe only a few minutes long. There are many opportunities for teaching moments. Think of a lunch and learn or an informal session with the goal to share insights among fellow Agile coaches. These are all opportunities for the coach to teach employees and teams elements of scientific thinking and the use of Agile Kata.

Agile Kata does not have roles or events. There are really no rules either. Applying Agile Kata is not about the four-step sequence but about the practices and tools that can be used to bring the sequence to life for Agile teams. Agile coaches look at all practices and techniques and how they relate to facilitation, mentoring, and professional coaching. They will assemble techniques and practices listed in the next chapter that can help Agile coaches create collaborative environments for Agile Kata teams to flourish.

The competency framework also contains three masteries: technical, business, and transformation. Considering that this framework serves Agile coaches in their personal growth and to identify strengths and weaknesses, those three masteries create new opportunities. Technical mastery can be seen as essential for Agile team coaches that work with software development teams. Transformation mastery was often reserved for enterprise Agile coaches, while business mastery focused on value streams and organizational effectiveness.

An Agile coach using Agile Kata will most likely work across all mastery levels and competencies, needs to be familiar with all of them, and is well rounded. Continuous improvement may touch many stances at the same time.

The growth wheel differs from the competency framework in that it includes additional stances that are surrounded by skills and eventually domain knowledge. In the center of the wheel is self-mastery. Do you live by the values yourself when you are in the role of an Agile coach? Do you portray an image that culturally reflects the environment you're trying to promote? Are you reflecting and learning yourself? The role of a second coach, discussed in Part I, can be of enormous value for Agile coaches striving to improve their skills and self-mastery.

Let's first take a look at the role of an Agile coach in general, and then I'll highlight individual stances outlined in the frameworks and how they relate to Agile Kata.

Role of an Agile Coach

In recent years, the role of an Agile coach came under scrutiny in many organizations. In many of these instances, the role of an Agile coach isn't well understood. One executive who was getting frustrated with the new ways of working asked me, "Please tell me what a scrum master does all day, except running a 15-minute stand-up." My response opened up a much deeper conversation about Agile ways of working, in this particular case with Scrum.

I started off by answering that the stand-up isn't an event the scrum masters would need to attend at all. I said they are actually optional. The executive was stunned to hear that. Then we unpacked the difference between what he called the *stand-up* and what the event is actually called, the *daily scrum*. For many, these terms became interchangeable, but there are important differences. The daily scrum is an event that intends to sync developers on the team around the current sprint goal. The goal is to quickly organize the next eight hours together and find ways to navigate closer to that goal. Scrum does not care, nor prescribe, if you stand or sit during that event. Standing up is certainly a popular technique, and it has been shown that the event can be shorter when people stand. But scrum neither enforces that as a rule nor requires "police" to support that behavior. The daily standup has its origin in Toyota, where in Japan all team members will have a daily meeting lasting 10 minutes, usually straight after lunchtime, to coordinate progress and planned work and to focus on improvement activities.

I have seen many cases where scrum masters would encourage a team every single day to get up from their chairs and build a circle. There were even instances were developers faced the scrum master like in a U shape. These are bad habits, but they demonstrate the misunderstandings about who is in charge and the overall purpose of the event. This is a small and detailed example, but it shows why learning through coaching is best when done continuously. Feedback and immediate correction of behavior is effective when done on the job. As efficient as initial classroom training can be to kick off learning and improving, especially for a group of people, it is the coaching that allows us to course-correct behavior before it turns into a bad habit.

Also, pause to think about how the daily scrum situation I described earlier would impact self-organization. What would happen when the scrum master is on vacation or is absent for a longer period of time? Would the event fall apart because the developers decide to skip it? Or would it continue because they see value in it? How do you think the scrum master feels in my example as they put their energy into rallying the team every single day? Who owns the process: the team or the Agile coach?

If someone's understanding of the role of an Agile coach is reduced to a person who runs a daily meeting every day, the concern about what they are being paid for is certainly justifiable. One root cause is often that the Agile coach is limited in their radius and can't demonstrate the skills of all the stances. That limits the role of an Agile coach and indirectly limits learning and growth. Robotic behavior and simply executing the process framework with its events, roles, artifacts, and rules does not remotely depict the vast playing field of an Agile coach.

In my daily scrum example, a simple question or statement can bring to surface some interesting discussions about servant leadership, self-organization, agility, and, in this case, a process framework. If you're working and facilitating the framework, instead of focusing on the people on the team and value, you will find a few use cases in Part III to give you some fresh new ideas and perspectives.

When using any of the two Agile coaching competency frameworks, you can better define what you would expect from Agile coaches in general, and in particular, when they are coaching teams in Agile Kata and scientific thinking.

Activity

In the State of Agile Coaching Report 2022,[7] the majority of Agile coaches (39 percent) responded that one of their challenges is the difficulty of changing mindsets and cultural shifts. Others state organizational structure (28 percent) and resistance from management (18 percent) as their challenge. Five statements and quotes from that report are in the following list. Based on your Agile Kata knowledge, how would you respond to these statements? Write down how Agile Kata would address them.

- Culture and mindset shift is the greatest challenge, especially with higher levels of leadership, due to a lack of direct engagement.

- Management has difficulty retaining an experimental mindset in the face of challenges.

- The command and control structures are deeply rooted, and it takes patience and time to mold individual mindsets.

- There are too many generals, too many North Stars.

- Executives tell us to be Agile but don't adjust their expectations accordingly.

Typical challenges of an Agile coach are not about implementing a specific process framework or tool. The biggest challenges are related to organizational change, culture, and leadership. This requires a closer look at the various stances of an Agile coach and how Agile coaches can apply Agile Kata and foster a culture of scientific thinking within each stance more effectively. Figure 6.3 shows that scientific thinking as a discipline impacts all skills and stances. But there is also the process of implementing and performing the practice of Agile Kata within the Agile/Lean Practices segment.

---

7. Produced by Scrum Alliance, ICAgile and Business Agility Institute

Figure 6.3
Growth wheel with scientific thinking (Agile Coaching Growth Wheel concept by Shannon Carter, Rickard Jones, Martin Lambert, Stacie Louie, Tom Reynolds, Rohit Ratan, Andre Rubin, Kubair Shirazee, and Mark Summers, licensed under CC BY-SA 4.0.)

For example, Lyssa Adkins[8] defines an Agile coach as someone whose "primary goal is fostering growth and transformation of Agile teams and organizations." An Agile coach is a multifaceted person who is a facilitator, coach, mentor, teacher, and change agent. Through these stances, an Agile coach is a guide who helps teams and organizations to adopt and improve agile practices. In this capacity, an Agile coach works at a team and organizational level and makes sure the Agile principles are understood and applied effectively.

On this level, an Agile coach incorporating Agile Kata to Agile coaches is a natural fit. The goal of focusing on growth, value, culture, and agile practices is in the DNA of continuous improvement and scientific thinking. One way of using the Agile coaching wheel as a tool for self-improvement is to overlay the wheel with a spider diagram (refer to Chapter 4).

---

8. [LA2010]

Let's look at some concrete examples of how Agile coaches using Agile Kata can upgrade their skills based on the stances. Figure 6.3 shows that scientific thinking becomes central to the role of all agile coaching, although it requires self-mastery. Professional coaching, mentoring, teaching, and facilitation will continue to be needed, but they must be viewed through the lens of scientific thinking. Chapter 7 focuses on collaboration techniques, but let's take an initial look through the lens of scientific thinking at professional coaching, mentoring, and teaching.

Professional Coaching

You're already familiar with kata coaching cycle if you read Chapter 3. It is a connection point between coach and coachee, often performed daily. The five Coaching Kata questions help facilitate the conversation between the coach and the coachee. To start the conversation, it is recommended you stick to the script and ask the questions as presented, in the order they're listed in Chapter 3. You can then mature to asking deeper questions within that structure. Later, when the approach and questions have become a new habit, you may want to explore other questions and other formats, including them in your professional coaching stance, for example.

Coaching is a partnership. Structured and thought-provoking conversations between the coach and the coachee aim to help the coachee achieve their full potential and meaningful change. There are many different tools coaches can use to bring structure to the conversation—GROW, CLEAR, or co-active coaching, to name a few. The professional arc, illustrated in Figure 6.4, is built with powerful questions. It is another popular way of performing a professional coaching conversation for Agile coaches. The arc is popularized by the ICF[9] and is a reason I will be using it as well.

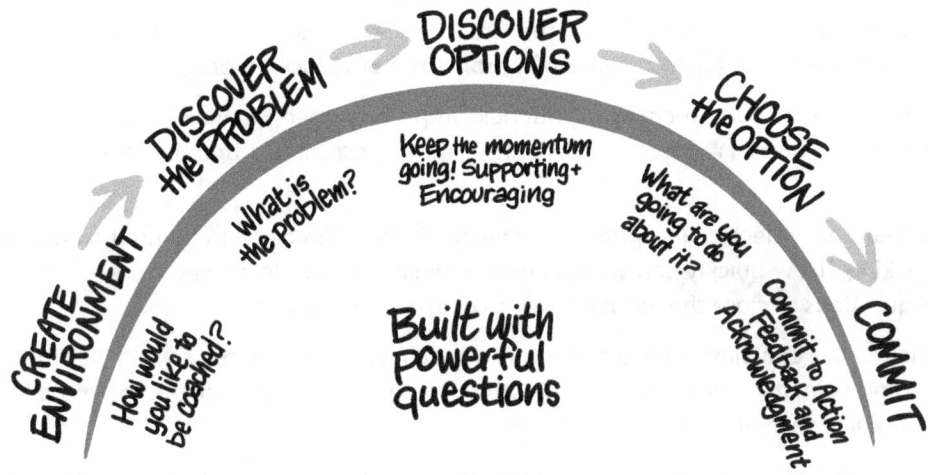

Figure 6.4
Professional coaching arc (Adapted from Coaching Agile Teams *(2010) by Lyssa Adkins.)*

---

9.   International Coaching Federation

Many Agile coaches use the arc for 1:1 professional coaching when they work with an individual to sharpen their skill set. This could be an individual team member or a leader. The coach guides the coachee through the arc, facilitating the five-step conversation from start to end. Ideally the conversation ends with a verbal commitment by the coachee about next steps. These conversations are typically short, depending on the topic at hand, anywhere between 15 minutes to an hour. Professional coaching is therefore a series of short coaching conversations. The frequency is determined and agreed upon by the coach and the coachee and may be adjusted over time. The sessions may not occur daily as the coachee may need extra time to follow through with experiments and actions, but they're also not spread out too much either. Mike Rother suggests trying to break down complex actions into pieces so something can be completed every day. Over time, the coachee navigates through personal change through practice, repetition, and, most important, on-the-job learning.

Although the arc is designed and works well for 1:1 coaching conversations, Agile coaches can also apply it to structure a conversation with an entire team. Instead of a more natural back-and-forth dialogue you would experience in a 1:1 conversation, the coach invites the team to have a brief conversation among the group and react to the powerful questions. Most important is that the entire team commits to something at the end of the arc.

The Coaching Kata questions are powerful. Agile coaches can easily integrate those five questions into the arc. For example, these three questions

- What is the target condition?

- What is the actual condition now?

- What are the obstacles you are addressing now?

all make great powerful questions during the "Discover the Problem" step. Identifying "obstacles" can help dig into the possible root cause of a problem that's blocking progress.

The question "What do you expect from your next step?" helps people think through why they're taking this action and may lead to considering more possibilities under the step "Discover Options."

Once the team has selected an option, the coach will take the team to commit to one of the options. Asking, "How quickly can we go and see what we have improved?" fits as one of the powerful questions to close the arc. It's a way to gain a commitment.

Integrating the five Coaching Kata questions into the coaching arc not only works well, but it can be the starting point for experimenting with other questions when you are getting more familiar with the original coaching cycle overall.

Following the arc has been an effective tool for Agile coaches for years. The Agile coaching competency framework contains professional coaching even as a stance. The arc is a tool to create an environment for professional coaching because the team is always in the driver's seat of the conversation. It provides a structure to guide the team through the conversation. For example, emotionally connecting with the team in the beginning of the arc in "create environment" helps set the stage for a better conversation to follow.

Following the arc should feel like a natural conversation that opens with a greeting and closes with a good-bye. And just like a regular conversation with friends, we connect emotionally to find out how everyone is doing at the beginning of a conversation, and we often commit at the end to next steps by asking something like, "So, we'll see each other tomorrow at my party?"

Activity: Practice the Professional Coaching Arc

1. Think of a series of powerful questions that support any of the five steps in the coaching arc and write them down. Maybe write two or three for each step.

1. Ask a friend or colleague to be a coachee (any professional issue they are currently facing) and perform and record the coaching conversation (audio only).

2. Reflect on your conversation, the questions, and the answers by listening to your recording.

Professional coaching is not life coaching. Should you encounter a situation where the conversation drifts away from a professional challenge to a personal challenge, stop the arc and refer the coachee to someone who is skilled having that kind of conversation.

Mentoring

In professional coaching, the Agile coach facilitates a conversation by asking powerful questions. In this case, the Agile coach facilities the coaching conversation. The opinion or expertise of the coach is not relevant. The coach stays neutral.

Mentoring differs from coaching because the mentor may inject an additional option into the conversation when the conversation is at the top of the arc in step 3—"Discover Options"—as shown in Figure 6.5.

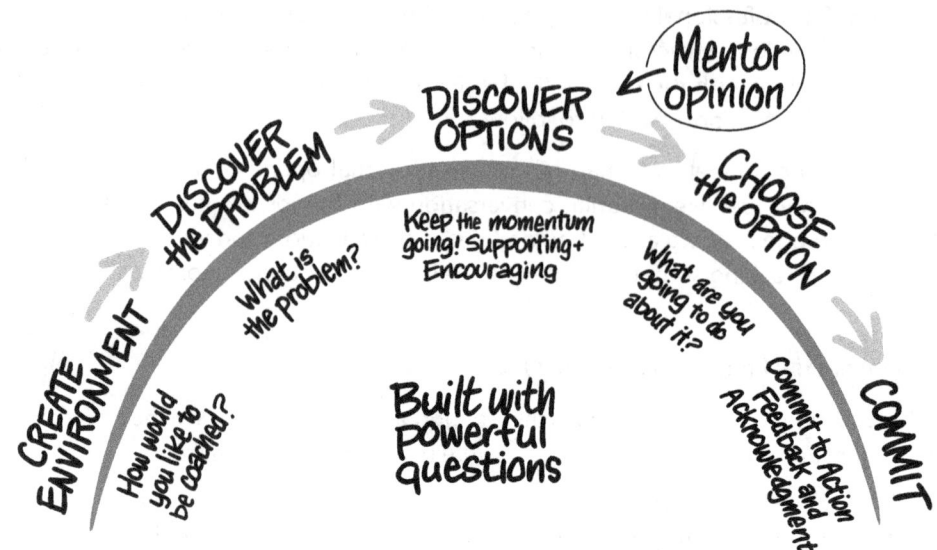

Figure 6.5
Mentoring conversation (Adapted from Coaching Agile Teams *(2010) by Lyssa Adkins.)*

As a mentor, you need to leave your ego at the door. Your role is to facilitate the mentoring conversation and, based on your experience, provide options to the conversation. Whether the team considers your idea and commits to it or decides to select an option of their own, it will be entirely their decision. The definition of mentoring is when someone shares their knowledge, skills, and experience with another person to help them to progress. You're here to facilitate the conversation and contribute with your expertise, not to direct and dictate what the team should do next.

Saying "I want you to try the following…" kills the energy of mentoring dialogue because the team isn't in the driver's seat. Don't assume that the team will immediately jump on your suggestion. They might see better value in an idea they generated. In fact, you should be pleased when the team learns to think for themselves. Remember that you're still providing value to the team as they identify a new idea as a result of the conversation you have facilitated, even if that idea isn't yours.

Instead of telling the team what they should try next, consider introducing an option by sharing a story. This story could stem from your experience or a metaphor like a fable,[10] for example.

As a general rule of thumb, I always recommend exploring options from the team before you inject your own. Be patient and comfortable with silence if needed.

---

10.   [JKHR2016]

Teaching

Let's explore another stance of an Agile coach: teaching. An Agile coach can fill many different stances and might slip back and forth between these stances within minutes depending on the situation they are in.

At Toyota, a teacher is more like a sensei. Whereas coaches at Toyota can coach and possibly teach line workers in their work, we don't typically see Agile coaches teach team members in a specific programming language. They coach them in agility and, now with Agile Kata, in scientific thinking.

Agile coaches work on improvements that have an impact on the organization. That is a drastic difference between manufacturing and knowledge work. Knowledge work finds itself more often in the complicated or complex domain in the Cynefin framework. That does not mean that manufacturing is simple, but it often has a component of repetition that Agile teams often don't have. Because of that, I think it is unrealistic to expect an Agile coach to become an expert in all the combined skills of a cross-functional team. That assumption changes how Agile coaches teach. We expect them to teach teams and organizations so that they can become more agile and scientific thinkers.

Teaching is knowledge transfer from the teacher to the individual or group. And even though effective learning happens on the job, teaching should be considered to be part of a learning strategy. You can think of courses as something performed in classrooms, a structured learning environment with exercises.

Teaching new drivers in driving schools how to open the car door better (see the Dutch Reach example I referred to in Part I) could be the first step in behavioral change. I'm emphasizing the first step here because the learning needs to be practiced afterward. Classroom training means having a group of professionals learning about a certain topic in a safe environment— for example, through group facilitating and group collaboration skills. All these could be examples to jump-start a group with a new topic. Classroom learning could kick off other ways of learning—for example, blended, immersive, spaced learning modules, or online self-paced. There are many ways and formats of teaching and learning.

Teaching does not necessarily imply formal course. It could mean that an expert software engineer teaches others in the organization new tips and tricks, maybe just for an hour during lunch time. In this case, the Agile coach enables a teaching environment by facilitating the teaching moment or teaches the software engineer new teaching skills. Teaching requires a learning strategy to find the most appropriate way of conveying knowledge from A to B.

In the context of Agile Kata, the coach can teach topics to spread the knowledge of Agile Kata and scientific thinking. As a result, they can weave these topics into a learning strategy to spread the knowledge about Agile Kata in an organization.

An Agile coach therefore becomes a crucial role for becoming a learning organization. As Satya Nadella (CEO of Microsoft) said about demonstrating a growth mindset, "Don't be a know-it-all. Be a learn-it-all."

Change Agent

I look at kata as a pattern. As patterns become habitual, you don't have to think so much about the process you'll follow and can focus on the content and how to creatively approach the problem. A scientific thinking pattern prevents prematurely jumping to solutions and assuming you're right rather than considering the facts. Recognizing and applying a pattern like Improvement Kata can tremendously increase the success rate of an approach.[11] The confidence level is higher. Compared to best practices, which are often generally accepted solutions that prescribe a specific implementation, the Improvement Kata pattern allows for the exploration of multiple solutions.

Patterns can be adapted and reused in different scenarios that share similar characteristics. Practicing Improvement Kata as learning a meta-skill. It is at a higher level than a particular skill to perform a task. Although you are also learning about techniques and practices that bring Agile Kata to life, they are not prescriptive. They are offered buffet-style based on your needs.

The same way software engineers have been using design patterns[12] for decades with the goal to increase maintainability of IT systems, change agents are looking for organizational change patterns to design a change strategy. A catalog of these organizational change patterns is defined in the books *Fearless Change*"[13] and *More Fearless Change.*[14]

Pattern books are not necessarily read from start to finish. Your hunt for the promising pattern would begin with the problem you're facing. For example, the fearless change patterns are grouped into the following sections that change agents commonly face:

- Strategize

- Information sharing and seek help

- Inspire others

- Target resistance

Based on the obstacle or challenge you are facing, you would zoom in to one of the categories to then find a collection of pattern descriptions that you can experiment with by using Agile Kata.

The beauty of patterns is that you can assemble a change management strategy by connecting these patterns to a series, rather than working one by one.

---

11.   [CA1979]

12.   [GHJV1995]

13.   [MMLR2005]

14.   [MMLR2015]

There are many different practices, models, and techniques to introducing change, such as John Kotter's eight-step Change Model, ADKAR, and Lean Change Management, just to name a few. For any of these models, reflect on the impact it may have on Agile values and principles. Many of these models are structured in phases, which may derail your iterative Agile thinking into old-habit sequential development.

Coaching Ethics

It is inevitable, but every coach will encounter a complex situation at some point in their coaching career that may push the boundaries of ethics. Taking a certain path may be ethically correct but hurt someone or be less efficient than a more expedient and less ethical approach. How do you react, behave, and represent the profession of Agile coaches in a situation like that?

The Agile Alliance has launched an initiative to address these concerns and offers a "code of ethical conduct"[15] to the community of Agile coaches. That code offers guidance when you face any of the following difficult decisions:

- How is the relationship between a coach and team impacted if the coach releases the latest team health check with senior management without the knowledge of the team?

- How can a team grow when an Agile coach does not grow themselves?

- How do I react if the coaching drifts from Agile conversation to something outside my Agile expertise?

- How is your Agile coaching impacted if you don't disclose existing relationships with third parties?

- How about any hidden agenda, even internally, when being assigned to a "special project"?

- Are you stepping in addressing a situation when the language between team members becomes inappropriate?

It requires courage to navigate certain coaching situations. But there is something Agile coaches can do themselves to elevate their profession and represent through the existing code of conduct a value system that is sustainable.

One of the nine elements of the code is "agreeing on boundaries," which is the next topic: the "coaching contract."

---

15. https://www.agilealliance.org/agile-coaching-code-of-ethical-conduct/

Coaching Contract

Chapter 4 takes a holistic view of all 12 principles. But what if the person signing your consulting contract is asking you to focus only on half of the principles and ignore the others?

As an Agile coach, this would be unethical, based on the conversation we had in the previous section. But the ethical piece is only one side of the coin. The bigger question is, are you setting boundaries for Agile coaching?

Defining the scope and goals for Agile coaching is a critical step. Including the code of ethical Agile coaching would also be a good idea for both parties—client and coach. By making a reference to the code of conduct, you're committed to the principles of the Agile Manifesto and to work with your client on their agenda, instead of your personal preferences. This will increase neutrality and reduce your bias when working with your team.

Another way of maintaining neutrality is to assess the current situation with your client before defining what the step forward could look like: a longer-term coaching goal, an assessment of the current situation, a small next step that includes coaching experiments. Doesn't that sound like the four steps of Improvement Kata?

Define what is part of your coaching assignment and what is important. Using Agile Kata to drive the coaching engagement can create additional trust. Trust emerges through transparency, boundaries, inspection, and adaption.

The International Coaching Federation (ICF) offers a generic template for coaches on their website. Please keep in mind that the ICF serves all types of coaches, not just Agile coaches. That template may be too elaborate and lengthy but can serve as a good starting point for a more traditional coaching agreement. Many Agile coaches feel that the template is too detailed. Is a lengthy coaching agreement serving you well if you don't know if everyone has read the document in its entirety? Even if everyone has read the document thoroughly, the results still may be blurry.

A more lightweight approach is following the so-called team canvas popularized by Alexey Ivanov and Dmitry Voloshchuk. Although the team canvas can be used for very different reasons and situations, I have successfully used it to facilitate the boundaries of Agile coaching assignments with teams. You can adjust the canvas based on your needs or use the existing sections in the context of Agile coaching. For example, the "Rules and Activities" section could be a great spot to list kata as the approach to Agile coaching. "Values" could serve as a reference to the Agile principles.

Agile Coaching Summary

There is widespread belief that coaching is central to becoming a learning organization. Just as in sports or any complex skill, coaches teach, encourage, give feedback, provide practice drills, and generally motivate each person to continually improve. Though there is a long tradition of coaching in many endeavors outside of business, this has not seemed to penetrate the business world.

In Agile, we have various leadership and facilitation roles, but too often they do not seem to be "coaching" in the traditional sense. There are various models of coaching, but perhaps they are a bit too complicated to translate into practice. Simply giving someone a model with characteristics or steps does not translate into actual behavior. We have referred to scientific thinking as something you learn by practicing, supported by a coach, until the basic pattern becomes a habit. Similarly, coaching is something you learn by practicing, similarly supported by a coach, until the basic patterns become a habit.

Rother's *Toyota Kata* includes starter kata for learners, Improvement Kata, and starter kata for coaches or Coaching Kata. Coaching starts with a simple five-question card. You can at first simply ask the questions of your coachee. You will find the coachee may not answer each question in a satisfactory way. Then you learn to ask deeper questions as follow-up questions. Over time, as the pattern becomes natural, you can create your own approach to coaching.

An Agile coach has always been a role with many facets. Practicing Agile Kata will add an additional stance of scientific thinking to the spectrum of successful Agile coaching. Applying Agile Kata also means that existing stances like teaching, mentoring, coaching, advising, and change agent are impacted and benefit from scientific thinking.

In the next chapter, I discuss a variety of techniques that coaches can introduce to facilitate healthy Agile collaboration among team members.

Reflection

- What differences do you recognize between your coaching to someone like a sports coach?

- How do you balance providing guidance and allowing teams to discover their own solutions?

- What stances are your primary responsibilities in your organization?

- How do you ensure that your coaching practices are teaching scientific thinking based on concrete evidence?

- How do you continue to hone and fine-tune your coaching skills and get feedback from others?

- How do you embody the Agile mindset in your own work and interactions with others?

- What changes would you need to make to your coaching style to align with the Agile Kata and scientific thinking?

- Can you tell one success story from a situation you have personally experienced where you improved because of someone coaching you that you can use as a metaphor for future coaching?

- How do you inspire teams, ask questions, explore new ideas, and test assumptions?

7

Collaboration

You can do some wild things when you apply Improvement Kata. This is by no means a flaw of Improvement Kata because it is a meta skill. An extreme example is when someone maliciously uses Improvement Kata to introduce micromanagement to their organization, although I hope common sense would prevent someone from doing something so counterproductive. But think of more subtle improvement efforts, where we have good intentions but traditional management habits accidentally creep back in. We know these habits can change quickly back to old ways of working, especially if the other side feels different or unfamiliar.

When improving agility, there are two major concerns for leaders, coaches, and change agents. First, we want to make sure that an Agile mindset will guide us when we try to reach our set challenges. Chapter 4 introduced that Agile mindset as a safeguard. Second, the practices we use to execute the Agile Kata pattern should resemble the culture we're trying to create. Without Agile collaboration practices, how can we expect an Agile culture to emerge? Falling back into old habits, in this case practices, is unfortunately a potential trap. Think about what message you are sending to your colleagues if you're not collaborating in Agile ways while transforming. This was so important to me that it became the subtitle of this book: *Patterns and Practices for Transformative Organizational Agility*.

Every time I helped clients at various steps of their Agile transformation, I incorporated one or more practices that helped enable agility. They are like role models that served me, and more importantly my clients, very well. *Practices* clearly have to *be practiced*; it's right there in the word. With Agile kata they need to be practiced deliberately. Many of these practices you have seen, participated in, or read about. Open Space is an example. Have you practiced Open Space frequently in your organization? I know of several companies that run this format weekly in their company. It eventually became a new habit.

I'm not asking you to use all of the practices in this chapter. These are just a few examples that have worked for me. You might have your own that achieve the same thing, which is great. Instead of adding an abundance of practices that may or may not apply for you, I will utilize my book website www.joekrebs.com/agile-kata-book to share more practices in the future.

I invite you to think about the opportunities these practices provide for each of the steps in the Agile Kata pattern sequence.

Goals, Challenges, and Learning Zone

Agile teams are fully self-managed and set their own goals, like in Scrum. Products have dead-lines and budgets, and various measures are used, but I often see people accepting business as usual: Keep the product development cycle going, make good progress, get decent customer feedback, and you'll be okay.

By contrast, for Agile Kata teams the challenge is bold, audacious, inspiring, and long term. Sometimes it's even hairy.[1] Teams navigate the unknown, and that has an impact on reaching a goal. You may reach a goal faster or slower than expected and not meet all aspects of the challenges. In my experience, the teams generally get farther than they would without the chal-lenge, and sometimes they exceed all expectations.

I'm not talking about a putting-a-man-on-the-moon moment here. I'm talking about leaving the comfort zone, which is certain and predictable, and rallying as a team to meet a given challenge. Mike Rother talks about moving from the comfort zone to the learning zone. Compared to the comfort zone, uncertainty increases in the learning zone. Therefore, a well-formulated challenge contains unknowns and uncertainties. In the beginning, as you begin practicing scientific think-ing and learn, expect more uncertainties. Being in the learning zone not only increases team engagement, but the challenge also gives the Agile team a sense of accomplishment after it has been reached. The zones may shift over time; they aren't static. A learning zone in the beginning of a career might become apparent and certain later, shifting into the comfort zone over time. It's a fluid model.

However, the panic zone is too hard for the learner. Team members in the panic zone feel overwhelmed, which results in disengagement. Spending an extended period of time in the panic zone will sooner or later lead to a burnout. On the opposite end, spending too long in

---

1. [JCJP2011]

the comfort zone will lead to a "bore out." Figure 7.1 shows the sweet spot for effective team collaboration, called the learning zone.

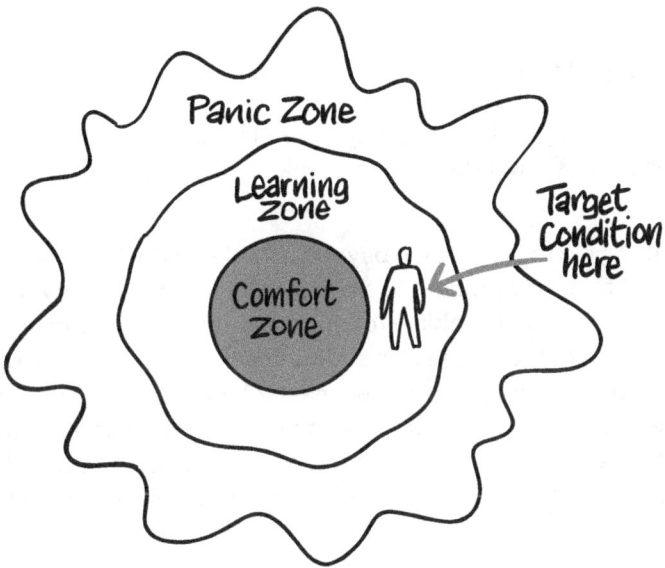

Figure 7.1
Comfort, learning, and panic zone (Adapted from Giving Wings to Her Team *(2023) by Tilo Schwarz and Jeffrey Liker.)*

Defining a challenge and creating a culture that embraces scientific thinking is therefore a crucial skill. Setting the right tone for the challenge and creating a culture of navigating the unknown is covered in Chapter 8.

Consider these questions:

- What are good ways of collaborating as a team to work toward these challenges?

- What are techniques and tools that work well for Agile teams?

- How can any of these techniques be used effectively when working in teams and applying scientific thinking in a group setting using Agile Kata?

- Which techniques have a strong influence and create an Agile culture while you're performing Agile Kata sequences?

- Which techniques have emerged as powerful tools that fit well with one or more steps in the Agile Kata routine?

In this chapter, we take a look at the characteristics of certain practices and techniques and why they make great candidates for Agile team collaboration, especially when used in combination with Agile Kata. I also strongly believe that these collaboration tools and practices are complementary to any Agile culture. Although they are not scientific, per se, they do create visibility of change.

Before teams can collaborate effectively, they need to form. The next section takes a look at team formation; later, I discuss collaboration techniques and practices.

Dynamic Reteaming

There was a time, especially in the early days of Agile adoptions, when many Agile coaches recommended that teams should stay together as long as possible. And there were some good reasons for doing that.

Stable teams meant staying together even beyond a single product development effort and possibly shifting as a unit from one product to the next. The reasons were typically about learning, trust, and collaboration but also the ability to forecast together. Ramping up a new product with a team that has worked together in the past sounded efficient. That was particularly true during the early days of Agile when the processes were new for many. A popular tactic was to train a team and keep them together. Shuffling up the teams often meant more training followed by more coaching. That has been seen as inefficient and costly by leaders. With the widespread introduction of Agile processes around the world, that aspect seems to be less of an issue anymore.

The one thing I learned during those early days was that keeping a team stable is an impossible task. Every organization has attrition, and employees often move within an organization based on their interest. U.S. employee tenure has steadily decreased since the 1970s at least partially because of the transition from being a manufacturing economy to a knowledge-working economy. With the higher degree of mobility created through technology, people can more easily jump to something that is more interesting to them.

Then there were times when organizations wanted to test Agile processes before they began investing more. Mixing team members with little to no knowledge about Agile into an existing team could have impacted those experiments. Back then, teams often chose a team name to build an even stronger boundary around them and between other teams, and that's less common today.

The current trends in the labor market, a stronger focus on knowledge work, and a broader understanding of Agile ways of working focus a spotlight back on team formation and, more importantly, reformation. Heidi Helfand calls this "dynamic reteaming"[2] and points out the advantages when changes to a team are intentional and strategic.

Dynamic reteaming begins with the idea that new team members are joining or leaving an existing team, but it doesn't stop there. Think about a team member in one team making themself available to join another team to learn something new or to bring in the existing skillset. This sounds very reasonable and commonsense, but some employees could fear repercussions when

---

2.   [HH2020]

they express an interest in leaving a team. That pushback could come from their existing team but also from their manager. In an environment with dynamic reteaming, leadership is in the driver's seat of creating a culture of changing teams on a regular basis.

Dynamic reteaming becomes especially interesting and important when product development efforts scale beyond a single team. For example, I was part of a program of 11 Agile teams, distributed across three continents and using either Scrum or Kanban as their team process. That was, however, not the way we started the program. We initially kicked off with 3 teams, grew quickly to 4, and then over time added several more teams until we peaked at 11. Once the product switched more to enhancement and maintenance mode, 2 teams were sufficient. Not only did the 9 teams focus on something new, but the remaining 2 teams also reshuffled based on their skills and the goals of the product. So instead of resisting change and keeping a team structure, dynamic reteaming encourages reformation and frequent change.

Dynamic reteaming is natural, organic, and logical. You can see in Figure 7.2 that the ecocycle shows the growth and renewal of teams.

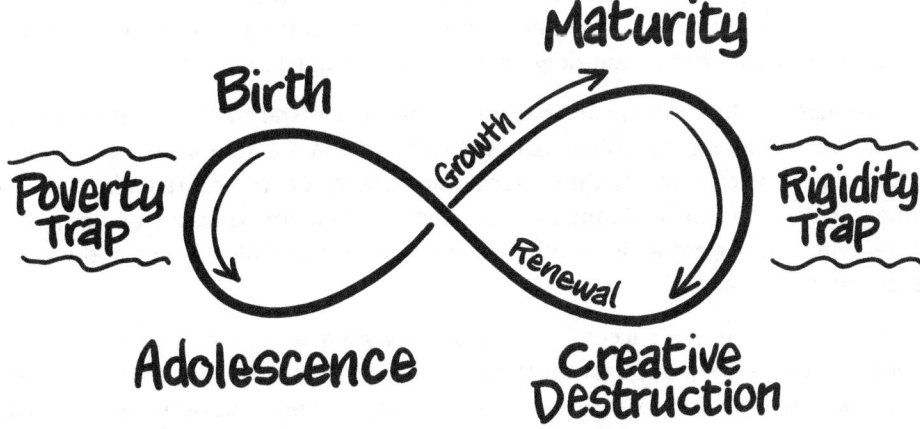

Figure 7.2
Team evolution ecocycle[3] (Adapted from The Surprising Power of Liberating Structures *by Keith McCandless and Henri Lipmanowicz.)*

But here is something I commonly face when working in traditional corporations where team formation is often seen as a leadership responsibility. Let's say you start with a new product, and you know it will take several small teams to divide and conquer. Many senior leaders and middle managers are tempted to make it their responsibility to organize people into teams. If they have 50 employees, and the goal is to break into teams not larger than 10, a typical answer is mathematical. In this case, they create 5 teams with 10 team members each.

---

3.   [HLKC2014]

Instead, an Agile mindset fosters a culture of self-organization and lets the team members decide on their own how they would like to build teams.

The team formations can be different than what you expect. For example, you might end up with fewer than 10 members on each team. You might have a team with more than 10 members, and maybe you'll have more than 5 teams. When you let teams organize organically, the results vary. Creating teams is about common sense, not a mathematical exercise.

To form teams in an effective, self-organized way, individuals need a clear goal and a room to meet (online or onsite). When they know the overall group of talent and the problem to be solved, they can organize themselves. It often takes only a fraction of time it would otherwise take to build teams in a self-organized way. More importantly, the teams have a totally different energy because the members chose their team themselves. This not only improves the speed of decision-making but also produces a higher-quality result. Let's look at why.

If a large group is to self-organize into smaller teams, each person considers the skillset they bring to the table and evaluates the skills from others that would choose the same group. In a global economy, they might also put time zones and office locations into consideration. And deep down, they might also pick a team with members they think they would enjoy working with. This is quite contrary to a top-down managerial approach.

Dynamic reteaming does not mean that organizations constantly shuffle their teams around just for the fun of it. They can follow patterns of team change or have periodic events where teams form.[4] Ad-hoc changes might be something you can accommodate, but you could also experiment with annual or semiannual events that offer reteaming opportunities. This is similar to transfer windows for professional athletes, when they can switch teams and join new clubs only a few times per year.

I know of one example of a successful Agile company where a manager organizes pairing. At Menlo Innovations, a frequent best-practice benchmark, they do 100 percent of their work in pairs, and they change pairs every week.[5] This is a requirement, not optional. A manager organizes the pairing, and you find out when you come to work Monday who you are paired with. The goal is to avoid what they call "towers of knowledge," and the process allows for a great deal of teaching and learning. They will tend to keep rotation for a big project within that project, and if there is a programming language used that some do not know, they tend to pair them with someone who knows the language. It's a very dynamic learning environment, and it shows that every company will discover their preferred way of working.

Dynamic reteaming and Agile Kata are a great combo. If you lose the benefit of team members staying together long term and developing solid connections as a team, what will tie them together? In Agile Kata, they have in common the mindset of scientific thinking. They have a

4.   *Agile.FM*, episode 118 with Chris Smith

5.   [RS2015]

common vocabulary, a common way of thinking about how to approach goal attainment, and a common way of thinking about experimenting. Rather than debate opinions, they discuss facts and choose to test out an idea they may disagree on. A team that focuses entirely on building an IT solution might require different stakeholders at various points during their work. It requires different expertise when the product being created cuts through different vertical business functions, such as procurement, finance, or marketing. Again, they share the common perspectives and vocabulary of scientific thinking, which becomes core to the company culture.

Team stagnation can also be a tough hurdle to pass when experimentation and habit change is important. When work becomes boring or repetitive, dynamic reteaming can be an instrument to shuffle things up and create a new lively environment again, as you saw in the extreme example of Menlo Innovation.

When you accept the fact that teams are transient, it can feel easier to focus on the challenge ahead. Agile teams using kata come together to reach a challenge, and because team reformation is possible, tension or conflict is less of a concern.

Dynamic reteaming can be a great enabler for teams practicing scientific thinking. Challenges are being addressed by dynamic transient teams that form around a given clear goal and smaller self-defined target conditions. Testing hypotheses through experiments may require additional stakeholders and team members who make themselves available as needed and are being added.

For larger organizations, the challenge is to enable an environment in which employees become aware of other employees' skills and expertise. To enable that, activities such as 1:1 walks, having lunch with someone you don't know, team member posters, and walking in my shoes are easy ways to create awareness about each other's interests and skills.

Pairing

Let's go back to the example of pairing at Menlo Innovations. Many Agile developers are familiar with pair programming. Two people, shoulder to shoulder, share one keyboard. Sharing one keyboard used to be the standard for this technique because the keyboard was the collaboration tool (Figure 7.3). Today, with more remote teams, you do see pairs where each person has their own laptop. Having your own keyboard creates more personal space, making everyone feel more comfortable because working shoulder to shoulder is not for everyone.

Figure 7.3
Pair programming

In another example, pairing is a common practice among police officers in Europe, especially in higher-risk situations such as night shifts, patrols, and work in urban areas. Elevated risk also means decision-making is more complex. Safety, back-up, better decision-making, and mental and emotional support are common benefits when police officers work in pairs. As a result, you typically see two officers in a car.

In programming, code review, coding standards, and knowledge sharing in both directions are key benefits. Just think of a maintenance or refactoring situation that occurs later in the development effort; at least two people have experience and can share insights about the code elements.

I can't tell you how many times executives have asked me why they should pay two people to do the job of one. I always reply that this technique is so powerful that they are paying two people to do the job of three. When working in pairs, people are usually very focused on the work at hand. In my experience, pairing is so intense, in a good way, that overtime is really not an option. At Menlo Innovations, after a day of pairing, people usually need a break and call it a day without working over.

Pairing has learning and productivity built in. If you decide to rotate pair partners every day or week, you cross-pollinate and learn even more. Rotation does not need to be rhythmic, but the more you do it, the more viewpoints are being considered when building the products. Say good-bye to knowledge silos and experts within a team.

To actively reduce the risk of knowledge silos, teams often use so-called pair-stairs (Figure 7.4) to visualize how many times team members have already paired with each other in a given time period.

Figure 7.4
Pair-stair

Even if team members build pairs for only a few hours every day, you will notice significant improvements in morale, quality, and performance. For example, one client of mine had so-called "pairing hours" between 10:00 a.m. and 12:00 p.m. and 2:00 p.m. and 4:00 p.m. every day. They were all working on-site in the same office location. During those hours, no team member would work alone. They set this as their own rule and did not allow any meetings. During pairing hours team members had to decline any meeting request. That ensured that each team member had quick access to another team member if needed for quick decision-making. Pairing hours were defined in the team agreements.

But the situation got a bit challenging when a highly ranked senior executive invited the entire team to a meeting during their pairing hours. As a result, each team member declined the requests within seconds of the others.

The senior leader felt hurt and mentioned to me that the team members' reactions were rude. He wanted to speak to me 1:1 in his office. The executive mentioned that "this Agile thing is ridiculous!" and he told me that if he wanted to meet with the team, the team should meet with him. It quickly became a power play.

Rejection like this hurts, no question, especially when it comes out of the blue. I represented the side of the team and what they wanted to achieve with this approach: increasing productivity by focusing on the product and each other during the pairing hours. I continued by telling him that the team didn't say "no" to the meeting; they just said "not now." They showed courage and followed their working agreement, which is an important element because it defines account-abilities and responsibilities among Agile team members.

I suggested the senior leader plan a meeting sometime between 12:00 p.m. and 2:00 p.m. and maybe even meet and pay for lunch. As a result of pair programming, that particular team had extremely high productivity, improved team morale, and overall client success.

Organizing in pairs can also be very beneficial for teams practicing scientific thinking with Agile Kata, especially when team members are testing a hypothesis through a series of experiments.

Pairing and regularly rotating pair partners can help encourage brainstorming among individuals, pairs, and the entire team. Organizing in pairs can be a huge advantage for Agile teams using kata, especially when they bridge the gap between the current and target conditions.

Mob Programming (Software Teaming)

What comes to your mind when you hear the word *mob*? I first had a negative association with it because it often describes a disorderly or unruly crowd, most likely the opposite of what a corporation might be looking for as their company culture.

In the context of Agile development practices, *mob* is quiet positive. Mob programming started off as a joke when Woody Zuill began working with a team that was looking for a team name.[6] Because the group was bigger than a pair, it became a mob. They called themselves the "mob programming" team. It was catchy and quirky and quickly caught on to describe a collaboration technique that has enjoyed more popularity in Agile organizations in recent years. Mob programming can be a great asset for Agile Kata teams in a variety of ways.

In recent years, even Woody Zuill began using the term *software teaming* instead of *mob programming*, whereas others prefer the term *ensemble programming*. These different names describe the same technique, so choose the one that fits your culture the best.

There are two very common questions you hear when someone wants to learn more about mob programming:

- What is a good size of a mob?

- How can a mob possibly be productive?

The size of a mob is variable; there is no rule or fixed number. Determining the best size of a mob begins by asking another question prior. Do you have the skills and knowledge to solve a certain problem? If you answer this question with a clear "yes," the problem is easy to solve. Then you don't need a mob at all. Just do it.

In knowledge work, a worker rarely has the skills and knowledge to build a feature of a product proficiently. I'm not talking about writing a line of code or doing another small granular task. That activity is coding and is only one of many steps in problem-solving. What has been coded needs to be tested. Does the person who has written the code also have all the skills and knowledge to do the testing? Most likely not. (I'm purposely ignoring the fact that a programmer

---

6. *Agile.FM*, episode 67 with Woody Zuill

should never test their own code anyway because it's not good to grade your own homework.) I'm talking about user interface design or any foreign technologies that might become part of the solution that can be very common for Agile Kata teams. That's where a mob comes into the mix. The big difference is that the members of the mob have a much bigger chance of solving the whole problem at hand—not just a small slice of it. And they'll be able to do it without hand-offs, which means no delays and less wait time. Why? Because mobs work collectively on the same item.

Problem-solving is neither linear nor a one-way street. Problem-solving requires a communication channel that is not only open both ways but also occurs frequently. The more fluidly communication can occur, the better it is in terms of efficiency and in the quality of the solution. Without a mob, you would have to schedule meetings and then more meetings to follow up on the previous meetings. That can cause tremendous delays in decision-making and overall speed of progress. One of the worst examples I can think of are so-called "alignment meetings" where people from various functions meet to realign. Those meetings are very expensive. Depending on your audience and time zone, they are not easy to schedule, and therefore slow down the cycle time even further, especially when they are done virtually. Those alignment meetings are not hands-on, not working sessions, and do not take place at the gemba. As a result, any decisions during such a meeting will most likely trigger more questions that require an additional alignment meeting. This is a very unnecessary vicious circle. What appears to be efficient coordination efforts is highly ineffective and costly.

Once members of the mob have been identified, the group size of a mob is still not final. At any given moment, when a situation arises that requires additional skills or knowledge that is not represented in the current mob, the mob size can be increased. Agile Kata teams can therefore be very flexible in their structure and how they approach experiments.

If members of the mob feel they are not adding value, they should leave the mob and focus on other activities where their knowledge is more valuable. That is of course common sense, but I believe it's still worth mentioning.

There is no waiting around in a mob. A mob takes away all that overhead by having the group collaborate for a short period of time (Figure 7.5). So instead of defining a fixed mob size, it is important to identify the people who are needed to solve the problem. But to give you a rough orientation, think of a group of about five to seven people, or slightly more, but keep in mind that coordination efforts increase when the mob becomes larger. Should you require a bigger mob, you are not violating any rules.

Figure 7.5
Mob programming

Mobbing does not mean that you are formally creating new teams multiple times each week because mobs are transient. Instead of lengthy planning activities and coordination efforts, why not assemble a mob that exists to work together? Maybe there are good reasons to keep the mob together for a follow-up activity, but that needs to be evaluated on a case-by-case basis. More typically, mobs dissolve or change—inspect and adapt.

Agile Kata intends to increase agility in a team or organization in general and is not limited to teams building software or IT solutions. Even though mob programing originated as a technique for software development teams, it can be useful for other teams, including teams that practice scientific thinking using kata.

Using mob programming techniques in a nonsoftware situation probably requires some adjustments. The idea is experimentation, just as it is in so many other situations. Industries are diverse, and so are product ideas. For that reason, mob programming needs to fit the environment, not the other way around. The shared (large) monitor or projector is ideal for software mobs because everyone can see the code and collaborate. In this case the code is the product, and the monitor represents the logical view of the product. Nonsoftware mobs might use a whiteboard, collaborative online tools, or even wall space—whatever works best for them in that situation. Think of a marketing mob or a mob that produces educational content. In nonsoftware mobs the roles of driver and navigator may rotate more frequently. The driver is the person with the keyboard who is writing and reviewing code. The navigator thinks more strategically and encourages facilitation and collaboration.

A mob focused on research and development might not need to be a full-time mob. It might make more sense for it to be a part-time mob that assembles for only a few hours a day. A mob focused on the preparation that's outside a software team becomes very important when increasing business agility is the goal. This would be similar to the pairing hours described in the previous section but applied on a mob level.

For Agile Kata, a mob fits with the planning and execution of experiments and therefore reaching the next target condition (step 4). Because of the potential to accelerate delivery by using mob programming over traditional ways of working, the combination of using mob programming with Agile Kata can make organizations reach their goals faster. As contradictory as this may sound, Agile Kata can give a mob a little bit of structure by focusing on a target and experimenting together.

I believe that mob programming can be a better fit for teams using Agile Kata than teams using a framework that uses time-boxing, such as Scrum. The nature and mindset of a mob is to reach a solution to a problem collectively and within the parameters of quality as fast as possible. This works especially well to bridge the gap between the current condition and the next target condition. On the other hand, time-boxed iterations require allocating work to time rather than to a target, as scientific thinking does.

Earlier, this chapter took a closer look at the opportunities and advantages of dynamic reteaming. You might ask yourself how that is different from mob programming. The focus of dynamic reteaming is organizational effectiveness, whereas mob programming focuses on being effective to solve a problem. Mob programming is about team cohesion and collaboration to complete work, whereas dynamic reteaming aims to foster innovation through changing team dynamics only a few times a year. Teams that reteam dynamically can still apply mob programming. But mob programming does not require dynamic reteaming. Those concepts coexist very well.

In summary, the term *mob programming* may be controversial, insensitive, or misleading, but the benefits should elevate a discussion of that technique beyond its name. Mob programming is simple, gets people with skills together, and has them focus on one issue at a time. Things will get done faster. It's not magic—just common sense.

Mob programming

- Reduces technical debt
- Improves quality and compliance with company standards and protocols
- Speeds up delivery times
- Reduces operating costs
- Lessens context switching
- Increases ownership
- Accelerates knowledge sharing and learning

These are all positive attributes for any Agile team, but when applied during experiments, which is at its core of the scientific thinking, it is a powerful technique.

Hackathon

The term *hackathon* is a combination of *hack* and *marathon*. In this case, *hack* isn't a reference to the activity of bypassing information security and possibly intruding on other systems and networks. Instead, *hack* has its origin in exploratory programming that encourages creativity, learning, and experimentation.

Blending the word *hack* with *marathon* emphasizes that this is an event that lasts from one day to a week. During that time, the group self-organizes into teams, and then they begin experimenting. Typically, teams start with some initial ideation before they begin testing these ideas by turning them into software. All that happens under the umbrella of a given goal that guides the participants of the hackathon. There is also typically a brief presentation about the goal, the logistics, and expectations of the hackathon. And just like in a regular marathon, there will be some winners and awards at the final ceremony.

In comparison to mobs, teams in a hackathon stay intact during the event. Hackathons are more occasional and sporadic events, whereas mobs are a practiced continuously. A hackathon also often results only in a working prototype, and it's most likely not an increment that can be released. The focus of a hackathon is to explore ideas and test their feasibility.

In my experience, a hackathon creates enormous energy and fresh new ideas. They are an adequate technique to test big, bold, audacious goals and can serve as a kick-off for a product. I have organized and facilitated hackathons privately (company-internal) and publicly during a conference. Both produced tremendous results in a short period of time. It felt as if the public hackathons generated more out-of-the-box ideas, which might be related to the fact that the teams were not bound by existing rules and guidelines of their company. On the other hand, employees have more skin in the game during a hackathon for their employer and evaluate the practicality of ideas and experiments beyond the initial hackathon.

A hackathon event starts with preregistration, when employees and other participants are asked to volunteer to join. For participants to make an educated decision as to whether they have the skillset to attend, the organizer shares the goals, resources, and schedule. Because there is a prize at the end of the hackathon, success criteria and information for the winners is shared upfront as well. Sometimes during the registration process the actual project teams are already formed. Because the participation between registration and kick-off often changes, teams are built in the beginning of the hackathon.

During that time, the facilitation of the event begins by sharing the agenda, format, and logistics. Maybe a speaker gives a short keynote to give the hackathon direction and general motivation.

I have seen instances where the hackathon is somewhat chaotic and leaderless, and it can lose focus. Because a hackathon naturally promotes exploration and experimentation and requires team decision-making under short time constraints, Agile Kata provides each project team in a hackathon with the structure, discipline, and process to work toward the hackathon's challenge. In this case, each team inside a hackathon uses Agile Kata to work toward the given challenge and rallies behind it. They then define small targets during the hackathon and organize experiments.

A storyboard is one starter kata that teams might find useful to create transparency of the experiments taken, their outcomes, and what was learned. The information on the storyboards can be of great value during periodic checkpoints, which typically occur during multiday hackathons. Instead of daily coaching cycles, teams in a hackathon may increase the frequency of coaching cycles to react quicker and meet the given time constraints. Beside a facilitator of the overall hackathon, a coach could work with each project team during the hackathon to promote self-organization, create transparency, and lead the coaching cycles.

As part of the team coaching, a coach may incorporate other powerful facilitation techniques. For example, a "shift and share" Liberating Structure could promote cross-team learning and carve out additional opportunities for innovation.

Hackathons are very focused, short events and can be a great tool to spark innovation in a product organization. The result can be a starting prototype or first step of a new product. The simplicity of the Agile Kata pattern aligns well with the format of a hackathon.

Open Space

Open Space[7] is a simple yet powerful facilitation method that can be used for small meetings or large group gatherings. I have successfully used and facilitated Open Space for events with up to 500 attendees. However, 500 attendees is not an official limit. An Open Space can be even bigger than that. At internal company events, using Open Space is even more powerful, as you will see in a moment.

Harrison Owen, creator of Open Space, had noticed that the most important conversations often took place in a hallway, in the coffee area, or at a water cooler, not in meeting rooms.

There are many great books that introduce the Open Space format from a facilitator's perspective, including the one from Harrison Owen himself. So instead of introducing the technique, I want to share a story from an internal Open Space with a client of mine as well as a visual that gives you a feeling of the style and energy of Open Space (Figure 7.6). It started when I was invited to a three-day global executive event for a large U.S. client that was scheduled two months out. I was fairly new to working with them. Most of the time, clients see me as a trusted advisor about Agile coaching and training. At first, I wasn't sure about my role in participating in this three-day annual event that had a predefined format and flow. The expectations were not clear to me, so I asked to learn more about my role in all that.

It turned out that each leader representing their country or region would have a short time slot to report on results, forecasts, and business challenges. The agenda was packed for all three days, but they had also assigned one of those time slots to me to educate people on the planned Agile transformation. The leadership team found that valuable because the Agile transformation would have either a direct or an indirect impact on all the global leaders in that meeting. During information gathering, I quickly learned in 1:1 conversations with individuals attending the event how they

---

7. [HO2008]

really felt about the upcoming event. I heard things like "Three days of PowerPoints are tiring," "This is one expensive event," but also, "The main value is that we all have a chance to meet and have dinner together." So instead of grabbing my 30-minute slot, I decided to explore alternatives, and I proposed an Open Space that would set the tone for working in Agile ways in the future. I thought there would be no better way to demonstrate the Agile mindset than using a totally new form of collaborating that would signal an immediate visible change—living the Agile transformation from day one.

Figure 7.6
Open Space

The leadership team wanted to know more about Open Space, and I began explaining the technique. They challenged me quickly with questions like, "You're telling us that there is no agenda going into an Open Space, just an empty marketplace that will be filled by the attendees?" or "People decide with their feet where they want to contribute?" I kept answering questions like that with "Yes!" But then I also heard concerns like, "What if nobody wants to do anything?" implying that the grown-up leaders and middle managers were otherwise taking an easy way out if there wasn't an agenda. It almost sounded as if the intended PowerPoint marathon was used to show the attendees that this was not a joy trip.

The person responsible for the success of the event was reluctant, to say the least: "We have always had that format. Everyone is used to it." But the biggest hurdle was the belief and anxiety that nobody in the room would add something to the empty agenda. I asked the organizer what the goal of the three-day gathering was, and I couldn't get a straight answer. We started to get closer to the source of the problem. With a large group of highly experienced people, we could easily solve bigger problems than just updating each other on our work.

Let's find out where the problems are. Open Space uses a theme for that, usually expressed as a question because the goal of the group is to find answers to those questions. For example, "How can we decrease the fulfillment time of our products?" tends to generate energy and creativity. Instead of listening to a PowerPoint update about a specific geographical territory far away, meeting participants are now feeling that their expertise is appreciated and that their opinion is valued because during an Open Space, we expect attendees to work on the items listed on the marketplace. Open Space is a collaborative, interactive event with results. The results might be concrete action items or items that require further exploration in a subsequent event. Carefully thinking about the theme is therefore crucial and might require a bit of time to craft. In this case, I was able to help the facilitator develop a theme and invitations.

Because the organizer was anxious of trying something new for such a costly and important gathering, it took me a few 1:1 meetings to show the benefits of Open Space and to convince my point of contact. At one point he said, "OK, I will give you one of the three days" for facilitating an Open Space. I congratulated him for his bravery and asked for the first day to be the Open Space. He agreed to that as well.

Weeks later, when the group walked into the room, they noticed circles of chairs, an empty marketplace, and the theme in big letters across the wall. In each corner of the room, I had flip charts prepared. In the center of the inner circle of chairs were markers and paper. I explained the rule and principles of Open Space and invited them to populate the marketplace with ideas, questions, and topics. There was no limit to the items; all they had to do was contribute to the theme. That's it. Each time slot on the marketplace (45 minutes each) had a bunch of breakout areas, which were the flip charts. That meant that we had several topics run in parallel. There was no assignment; everybody could just decide where they wanted to contribute.

Within minutes, people got up, knelt on the floor with a marker in their hand, and wrote topics on the paper. They announced their topic and placed it on the marketplace. After the marketplace was 80 percent filled in less than 15 minutes, I told everyone that if new ideas came up, they could keep adding them to the marketplace, which was always open for new ideas. If we needed more breakout areas, we could arrange for that, too.

At that point, I took a more passive role and facilitated the event, enabling the group and keeping the marketplace up to date and transparent for everyone to see. I told everyone to regroup at the end of the day in the closing circle again. I am sure you already have an idea what happened during that closing circle. Correct! The group loved the format. They scrapped the agenda for days 2 and 3 and asked to continue with Open Space for the remaining time. On a day 3, someone showed tears of joy during the closing circle. When we moved the talking stick around in the closing circle, the person simply stated, "I have never been part of a more productive and fun meeting." The reason I know Open Space will work for you as well is simple: because it has worked so far every single time I've facilitated or participated in one.

When you're trying to introduce Agile ways of working to your organization but you keep the same events and facilitations styles, change is not visible. With Open Space it is. How could you expect a flourishing Agile culture and keep running the same meeting format over and over again? It just does not make sense.

Although Open Space is not a one-size fits all facilitation technique that should be blindly adopted for any meeting, it has found a wide range of application in the Agile community. Open Space has it all—self-organization, creativity, collaboration, networking, and problem-solving—which have great alignment with the Agile principles. As a result, Open Space is not only popular among Agile teams but can also support teams applying Agile Kata.

In terms of scientific thinking and Agile Kata, I see Open Space as a wonderful fit when leaders define a direction (step 1) or a target condition or when teams design their experiments. Shorter Open Spaces that last a half day or so might be sufficient. Open Space is by design unstructured, but scientific thinking can provide the minimal structure needed to help the group focus on achieving measurable goals. For example, it may not make sense to start with a big challenge for Open Space since it is of limited time duration, and we want creativity in defining goals. So perhaps the team can define a goal after some time pondering issues.

Mike Rother recommends the experimenting record plus a goal as a powerful way of keeping the group focused on experimenting while keeping them free to use a flexible approach to how they work. As enough individuals start to think scientifically, the starter kata may not be needed at all. The group will naturally start to ask questions like the following:

- What is our target condition?
- What idea are we testing?
- What did we learn from doing that?

Open Space is one of the 33 Liberating Structures, which I discuss in the next section, but I found Open Space so instrumental and powerful that I singled it out and made it its own section in this chapter. So, let's take a look at the other Liberating Structures and their benefits when working in Agile teams and practicing Agile Kata.

Liberating Structures

Liberating Structures are designed to increase team collaboration, engagement, and creativity within groups and organizations. Important elements are that all participants can contribute and bring their ideas into the mix. Decisions are made collectivity as a group in an inclusive manner. Liberating Structures give every person on a team a voice, and because there is zero threat to contribute and bring ideas to surface, they are a great way to maintain psychological safety.

Because of the well-known book *The Surprising Power of Liberating Structures*,[8] many facilitators may think that Liberating Structures are only 33 micro facilitation techniques. They're not. The book did a wonderful job putting the topic on the map for many facilitators, coaches, scrum masters, and change agents alike, and they serve as a great source of inspiration for helping Agile teams navigate scientific thinking. Those 33 made it into the book, but there are many other techniques to be explored and discovered. Because the Liberating Structures also come in the form of a mobile app, facilitators can always have them in their back pocket.

Why do I know they work, and why am I confident they will work for you? I remember a specific moment as a trainer nearly 10 years before the *Liberating Structures* book hit the shelves. I was with a client in the U.S. Midwest facilitating a training session. At one point in the training, I wanted to increase more collaboration and cross-pollination of ideas between groups that were working independently. This was a popular technique that I incorporated into group activities in classrooms quite often.

It began by asking the person in each group that was holding the flip chart marker at that time to stay with their group's work. Others of the group had a chance to maneuver as a unit clockwise in the classroom to the next group. The traveling group members could ask questions to the person who stayed behind. Neither writing nor critique were allowed, only inquiry and learning about the other's group's work in progress. Every three to five minutes, I gave a signal to move to the next station until the traveling group members arrived back home to their own work. Then it was time to share what they had learned from the other groups and revise their own work as needed.

What I didn't know was that exactly while I was performing this activity, a group of senior executives were touring the training space. Later that day, I was told that they were struck by the very positive energy and collaboration in the room that they'd observed from the outside through the windows and doors. The noise, interaction, and movement of people left a positive impression with the leaders of the organization, not to mention that the participants had smiles on their face. Even though the executive team had no idea what was going on in the room or the topic of the training, they picked up on the high engagement level in the room.

Much later, when the *Liberating Structures* book was published, I found this homegrown technique, which I had learned from other trainers, included as one of the 33 Liberating Structures under the name "shift and share." This is testament that the techniques that have an impact on

---

8. [HLKC2014]

positive collaboration stick and continue to live. Your techniques, although they're not already published in the book, could work for many others.

Before I get into the broader idea and use of Liberating Structures, I want to look at 5 of the original 33 Liberating Structures in the book and how you can possibly incorporate them into your daily work as a team facilitator. The following 5 stand as examples for all 33:

- Troika Consulting, great for exploring challenges or obstacles.

- 15% Solutions to identify a small next step during an experiment or implement entire experiments.

- Wicked Questions to challenge assumptions and stimulate critical thinking. These questions can help uncover underlying issues or assumptions or to identify areas for improvement and experimentation.

- Ecocycle Planning can be the starting point of an Agile Kata—for example, identifying areas of decline or stagnation of Agile practices in an organization. The combination of ecocycle planning and Agile Kata can keep your Agile culture fresh and effective (refer to Figure 7.2).

- Min-Spec helps teams stay focused on essential improvement ideas and can streamline decision-making and prioritization within the group applying Agile Kata.

All Liberating Structures are a great way to generate a higher degree of collaboration. They enable self-management and team autonomy and encourage teams to maintain a constant level of curiosity that will lead to creativity and innovation. All of these micro-facilitation techniques are therefore a facilitator's dream when performing Agile Kata.

The goal is not to work the Liberating Structures as a checklist to make sure you use them all. They are at your fingertips when you are looking for ways to decide quickly as a team about the next experiment or reflecting on a past experiment. Working in Agile teams differs from working 1:1 between a coach and learner. It requires team decisions and facilitation. Any of the Liberating Structures can help you organize that conversation.

Micro-Facilitation Techniques

Liberating Structures are not the only format that should be considered to increase engagement in a group setting. Just because one specific micro-facilitation technique did not make it into *The Surprising Power of Liberating Structures* does not mean that there aren't more out there.

Lean Coffee is a great example for that. In the context of Agile Kata, a Lean Coffee could help facilitate a discussion with the goal of determining a new direction or target condition or to discuss potential approaches to an experiment. Lean Coffee also generally works very well with learning and sharing knowledge as a group, which can come in handy with Agile Kata teams.

To give you a feeling of the abundance of techniques facilitators can incorporate into their toolbox that aren't listed in the book but still enable Agile ways of collaborating, here are some examples:

- Dynamic Facilitation
- Mind-mapping
- Action Learning Sets
- Solutions Focus Brief Theory
- Scenario Planning

But even beyond the popular and well-defined Liberating Structures, you might create your own over time through variations and riffs, just like the shift and share story I shared earlier in this chapter. For example, I frequently use *silent grouping* activities in my courses, where participants sort, order, and categorize the group work in a nonverbal activity. Time will tell if the technique will grow in the facilitators community.

Just because a technique is not known or has no name does not mean that it is not a Liberating Structure that could support a team when performing Agile Kata. Agile coaches also embrace experimentation, testing, fine-tuning, and determining new facilitation techniques over time and learning what works for their teams.

Facilitators are always on the lookout for new ways of engaging groups. Over time, you will recognize patterns in existing techniques that work better than others. Sometimes, finding real jewels in the crowded space of facilitating techniques is not easy or obvious. For example, the first time I saw the title of the book *Moving Beyond Icebreakers* by Stanley Pollack,[9] the word *icebreakers* derailed me. In reality, this book is a great source of techniques that can take a group beyond trivial icebreakers to a deeper experience. Even though books like these don't use words like *Liberating Structures*, they can help you design your techniques or variations.

Techniques that support teams in their path to their challenge in Agile ways are key ingredients. Being able to include everyone and hear all voices in idea generation and decision-making is crucial for success. But even more important is that by choosing these modern facilitation techniques over traditional meeting formats, change becomes real and is practiced and experienced as a group. Incorporating them often in daily routines with Agile Kata teams, these modern collaboration techniques help shift a culture of agility visibly.

---

9. [SP2005]

Collaboration Summary

Changing to an Agile mindset happens by creating new structures and connections in our brains. The way humans learn and change habits is an ongoing effort that happens at each person's own pace.

Working in teams requires certain social and personal skills to collaborate effectively. The Agile practices and tools introduced in this chapter can help teams to do that while upholding values that align well with an Agile culture.

Just learning about Agile processes but keeping the same old techniques is not a visible sign of change. Driving change with modern collaboration techniques will have an immediate impact on your success.

In this chapter, you got to know techniques that support a culture of self-organization, self-management, autonomy, and ownership. I'm not suggesting you need to apply all of them, and you can certainly be Agile without any of those introduced here.

My goal was to show you examples that have worked for me and many others very well. The examples I shared made change clearly visible inside and outside the team. Those techniques are hands-on, so they're effective at changing old habits, especially if you frequently repeat them. They might feel weird at first, but just like learning to ride a bike, they will become second nature soon.

I'm inviting you to experiment with the techniques whenever you see an opportunity. If you're an Agile coach, learn and use them. As a leader, create an environment for them and support them. As a team member, ask for them.

I also recommend stepping back and reflecting on the techniques currently used. Is each format enabling an Agile mindset, or are they counterproductive to the culture you're creating? Hold on, wasn't that already a reflection question? Here are a few more.

Reflection

- How can you create a culture of psychological safety for all team members?
- Based on your experience, can you describe a situation where you observed effective team collaboration? What were the key factors?
- Which of the techniques described in this chapter created the most interest or curiosity for you? Why?
- Can you describe one action you can do to increase collaboration that does not require permission or approval from somebody else?
- What can you do to mitigate any resistance to new collaboration formats?
- What steps can you take to increase collaboration in remote or hybrid teams?

8

Leadership and Culture

So far in Part II, I've discussed a few situations where employees faced challenges in their role as an Agile coach, facilitator, or team member. I talked about the impact of key performance indicators that focus on output rather than value. I shared that companies around the world face challenges when they begin cultivating an Agile mindset. You also got to know employees who followed protocol with terrible consequences. You got to know an Agile coach whose role was entirely misunderstood and reduced to something so basic that his existence was questioned. And, of course, I gave the example of the group of business development executives who had an annual meeting marathon that everyone was dreading.

But you also saw tears of joy when employees experienced Open Space for the very first time in their lives and executives whose jaws dropped when they saw a high-energy and productive training environment. I introduced you to a group of creative employees who applied common sense and out-of-the-box thinking to a business challenge. Not only were they able to do it, but it also saved their company.

My question to you, the reader, is this: Which of the two environments would you like to work in?

The difference between the two scenarios is leadership. Leaders create the playing field for others to perform. But what if the field is too small or too crowded? What do employees need to be creative, driven, and fulfilled? How can leaders create an environment in which others can be agile? Some of today's leaders have worked themselves "up" on the org-chart over the years, and they believe that they still know how the work on the ground is performed. As a result, micromanagement may creep in. Others lack trust and use power tools to direct and control. If you end up in a situation like that, you're at a dead end. And as Marcus Buckingham and Curt Coffman once summed it up, "People leave managers, not companies."[1]

When employees are treated like adults, they act like adults. Everyone makes incredibly big decisions in their personal lives, many of which are bigger than what they encounter at work. Examples include personal decisions such as who to marry, where to live, or what house to purchase. Pretty big decisions, if you ask me.

Why do we assume that a person who is willing to make big decisions in their personal life would like to work in a company that is making all the decisions for them? Not only is that demoralizing for the individual, but it's also slow and less effective for the organization. It's a no-win situation.

You might recall that earlier in the book I mentioned that 48 percent of leaders responded that changing to an Agile culture was their number one reason for failure.[2] Considering 76 percent of all Agile transformations have not reached their goals in the first place, this is a huge number of failures. But also recall the Gallup survey where a shockingly low 18 percent of U.S. employees said their organization is Agile, despite investing hundreds of millions of dollars into transitioning to Agile globally. There is no way to tiptoe around this very common issue; it is related to Agile leadership.

It also seems that the large majority of leaders believe in agility. Everyone wants agility, but they don't know how to change to it. What are the leadership skills that enable true agility? And, in the context of this book, how can leaders refresh agility in their organizations and send a new impulse by using Agile Kata? What are some ways to show that they are serious about their path taken? Some might get the wrong impression that Agile is dead in their organization, when in reality, they may have only reached a dead end. It's time to turn around and try something new. New paths are created by walking in a new direction.

Goals and Challenges

When I got to know the Toyota Kata, there were many things that fascinated me about the core Improvement Kata pattern, but the one thing that stood out immediately and connected the dots between scientific thinking and Agile leadership was the definition of a challenge. IDEO,[3] one of the most influential product design companies in the world, is very vocal about not being the expert in the products they are creating. Instead, they're experts in the process and how they approach problems. And yes, they are really good at it.

Teams need direction, a North Star that will guide them. Just letting teams innovate and create amazing products is vague. Giving teams a direction, which gives broad context, can gener-

---

1.   [MBCC1999]

2.   https://www.raconteur.net/report/agile-business-2022

3.   https://www.ideo.com/

ate energy, motivation, and engagement. Here's an example: "A new procurement system that supports a redesigned vendor management process to reduce onboarding time by 25 percent or more." Defining a challenge is a leadership skill. The Agile team needs a goal they can rally around. How leaders create the challenges differs across organizations. Goals must be sufficiently challenging but also achievable in a reasonable time frame. A goal that is too hard to reach results in apathy. A goal that is too easy to achieve will not sustain interest and engagement. Unless the company is very small in size, I would expect it to be a team effort.

In the example in the preceding paragraph, Agile teams would self-organize around the given challenge and aim to solve it. That means meeting or even exceeding the 25-percent target, but what if they don't reach the challenge and only achieve 22 percent improvement? Interestingly, I have never met a leadership team or product managers who were unhappy when teams improved a situation a lot, even if they did not meet the original challenge exactly. Of course, teams will push themselves to solve a challenge, but that is not always possible or desirable. Think of the costs it might take to improve the remaining 3 percent in the example. The question remains as to how agile leaders react in a situation when the challenges are partially met. Do they blame the team for not reaching their initial goal of 25 percent, or do they acknowledge that they made a huge difference by improving 22 percent? How do leaders react if the challenge cannot be met at all? Did they set an unrealistic goal?

Step 1 in Improvement Kata is defining the challenge to provide a longer-term direction for the team. This is commonly done in groups rather than in isolation, but it is the starting point for managing expectations. Challenges might shift and directions change. Challenges are moving targets, and redefining the direction may become necessary. Ideally, Agile leaders step away after they have defined what is needed and let the teams focus on how to do it. Continuing with Improvement Kata sequence, the team will then assess where they are (step 2), define a small target (step 3) and experiment to get there (step 4). It is the iterative process I describe in Part I.

Wait a second! Isn't that what the relationship between a product owner and developers is, too? Yes, but there are differences. The product owner and the developers are part of the same Scrum team. This means the Scrum team is self-managed as they define and solve a problem as a team. In Agile Kata, the leaders are external to the Agile team; therefore, the Agile teams self-organize around a given problem. Instead of spoon-feeding small items to a team, leaders create a bold challenge for the team.

These are not just semantics. I have seen many Scrum teams turn into feature factories. Product owners bring order to a product backlog and, by doing so, indicate what is next on the list. Then developers take items from the product backlog on one side and spit them out at the other side of the sprint. This is not what Scrum should be like, but unfortunately, that is something I have often observed.

Around the same time I began coaching an existing Scrum team that had been working together for quite some time, they were about to enter sprint review. The product owner decided to bring stakeholders along, and the developers showed the results of what they had been working on during that sprint. I remember the meeting was low in energy with the developers going through item by item, like a checklist. Then, in the middle of the meeting, one of the stakeholders spoke up and asked to pause for second. He wanted to congratulate the team for finishing an item that seemed very important to him. He said, "Guys, this is awesome. Do you have any idea how important this feature is for our business? This saves people a lot of time per week. Not to mention how tedious and annoying this task was. Thank you! Workers can now focus on more important things."

The developers had no idea whether the feature was significant or had impact to the business. Without that stakeholder in the room that day, they would have probably never known. In response to that comment, the energy in the sprint review changed immediately. The developers smiled, and it was easy to sense their pride. As a result, they changed the way they wanted to perform sprint planning going forward, gaining more context about the individual items before they began working on it. If there is no why or description of the value, then don't expect the level of commitment and engagement you desire from the team. Give them a real purpose!

In 2020, Scrum introduced a product goal, a commitment associated with the product backlog, to provide a product direction. In Scrum, product goals are very important and mandatory based on the Scrum Guide. Many Scrum teams have, unfortunately, no good answers when you inquire about the product goal. The longer-term vision is often missing in general.

In Agile Kata, defining the challenge (step 1) is an integral part of the process. Leaders external to the Agile team define it. Without it, Agile teams can't assess their current condition (step 2), define a target (step 3), or decide on experiments (step 4). The direction provides a tremendous focus before an Agile team begins working on anything.

Defining the challenge is by far not the only part leaders connect with teams during Agile Kata. Leaders make resources and people available so that Agile Kata teams can effectively collaborate, assess their current condition, and support their experiments. They create an environment for teams to be productive and help resolve organizational impediments.

Leaders strive to convert their company to become an Agile organization. But what is an Agile organization? And what skills are needed to lead through this change? Let's find answers to those questions next.

What Is an Agile Organization?

As we look at Agile leaders who initiate and support an Agile change culture, it's important to take a closer look at the goal of transforming. What does a future Agile organization look like? What behavior is expected? It's not surprising that the conclusions from surveys made over the years can be directly linked to scientific thinking and the Agile Kata.

The Agile tribe at McKinsey released a report of "The 5 Trademarks of Agile Organizations":

1. North Star embodied across the entire organization (defining a challenge)

2. Network of empowered teams (dynamic reteaming, mob programming, pairs)

3. Rapid decisions and learning cycles (one experiment at a time)

4. Dynamic people model that ignites passion (no rules, focus on targets, self-organization)

5. Next-generation enabling technology[4]

You might ask what the last item, "next-generation enabling technology," has in common with Agile Kata and scientific thinking. Think of operational excellence and the need for experimenting with emerging technologies.

Deloitte provided orientation for organizations by providing six criteria for "The Adaptable Organization":

1. Purpose driven

2. Customer-focused ecosystem

3. Flexible network of teams

4. Agile ways of working

5. Individualized talent management

6. Continuous change and learning[5]

As an industry, people have been discussing Agile culture, mindsets, and transformations for quite some time. You can tell from both reports, released in 2018, that many change agents feel far away from these desired states. Remember the Gallup study mentioned earlier in this chapter that stated that only 18 percent of U.S. employees say their company is Agile? Gallup continues to say that only one in five employees strongly agree that they feel a connection to their organization's culture. It appears that the goals, desires, and direction are defined, but leaders don't have the tools to implement that cultural shift. Agile Kata is here to help.

---

4. McKinsey & Company, January 2018 (https://www.mckinsey.com/capabilities/people-and-organizational-performance/our-insights/the-five-trademarks-of-agile-organizations)

5. Deloitte, 2018 (https://www.deloitte.com/global/en/services/consulting/services/future-belongs-adaptable.html)

Introducing Change with Agile Kata

Agile Kata is a pattern for driving change toward more agility. In previous chapters, I've already shown you that it is not a start-to-finish process. When getting started with Agile Kata and getting serious about scientific thinking, what can leaders do to increase the success rate of agility? Here are five concrete items leaders can focus on to initiate change with Agile Kata and make it stick:

- **Create a collective purpose:** Instead of delegating continuous improvement, identify a shared problem that can serve as a direction. By doing this, you are giving the organization focus and a reason for teams to support the mission.

- **Mindset over process:** Instead of seeing the transformation as a process, cultivate the mindset of scientific thinking. Agile Kata is a starting point, and your practices need to evolve. The goal is to become better in getting better, not simply to apply the same process for a long period of time.

- **Be flexible:** Stay flexible in the interpretation of practices, tools, and framework. Agile Kata is a compass, not a map. Stay true to scientific thinking and all Agile values and principles. Don't negotiate those.

- **Relationships:** Fight the habit of using a command-and-control management style. Foster personal relationships with peers and team members. Visit the gemba, participate in coaching cycles, and learn about the challenges on the ground. Then support the team or individuals in their actions.

- **Maintain focus:** Once a direction has been identified, let the teams self-organize. Don't create additional and possibly conflicting goals in parallel. Don't overload the system of change. Avoid team multitasking and having people work on multiple improvements at the same time. Don't ask for too much change too quickly; prioritize your improvements.

Now that you know the key characteristics of an Agile organization and have Agile Kata as a pattern for how to get there, I want to explore concrete leadership skills every Agile leader should demonstrate:

- Desire for facts and decision-making

- Creation of a learning organization

- Action orientation and supporting many small changes

- Sense of inquiry and seeking the perspective of others to navigate the learning zone

- Persistence in continuous improvement

Servant Leadership

When I deliver Agile leadership courses, I often take existing organizational charts and turn them upside down, as shown in Figure 8.1. I put the CEO at the bottom and the team members on the top. That often brings out interesting conversations about leadership styles. Of course, my goal is to provoke a conversation about the differences and create discomfort among the participants to generate new perspectives.

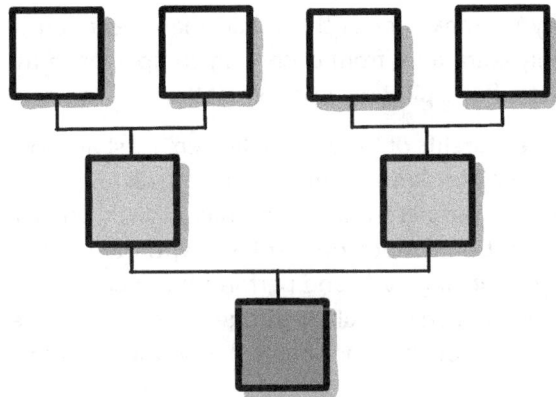

Figure 8.1
Flipped org chart

When I then talk about servant leadership[6] and the question "who serves whom?" the flipped org chart suddenly makes a ton of sense. The team members at the highest level create the product hands-on in cross-functional teams. The next level down, let's say middle managers, serve the teams to allow them to focus on building the product. And at the bottom, just before the C-suite at the lowest level in the depiction, senior managers serve the middle managers.

Every time I present this topic this way, I gain instant agreement. It makes total sense, and everyone agrees that focusing all energy on building amazing products for their clients is key. When asked if that is the way they spend their energy, they often smile and shake their heads. Why is that? What are they focusing their energy on? Status reports, time sheets, vacation plans, consolidating team metrics, preparing presentations, and so on. Most of these tasks require the lower level to be involved. As a result, team members are pulled away from building these amazing products for the clients because of existing habits at all levels of an organization.

The leadership style at Tesla and SpaceX is probably very different compared to what you have seen or experienced so far, at least according to what we hear about them in the media. Those companies have flat hierarchies and an all-hands on-deck culture regardless of the seniority of employees. At these companies, it is expected that everyone pitches in. For example, when a

---

6.   [RG1977]

truck needs to be unloaded at the loading ramp and there is a lack of personnel to do that at that time, everyone helps, even if that task is way outside of the person's job description. Unloading a truck could delay production of cars, which directly links to a negative client experience. Instead of a blame game of who is responsible for the fact there is a lack of personnel to unload a truck, an all-hands-on-deck approach is enforced across the entire organization.

This extreme focus on value, the client, and products resonates well with the approach Agile Kata teams would take: a group of senior leaders defining the challenge and then providing any support possible so that the teams can focus on the experiment by navigating in small steps toward that challenge. By no means does this mean that every company should be run like Tesla, but you can certainly learn a lot from observing companies in their approach to solving problems. Never copy; just take inspiration. Context matters.

Now that you have seen the benefits of the servant leadership style, how can you use Agile Kata to increase servant leadership? Looking at some of the characteristics of servant leaders[7] such as empathy, active listening, awareness, and community growth, you can notice how Coaching Kata can help leaders connect on a much deeper level with the team. Even if it is not possible for a leader to facilitate the coaching cycle and perform the coaching cycle with the Agile team, participating to learn servant leadership skills is a huge opportunity. Where else would you learn about impediments or issues if not from the source during the coaching cycle?

What obstacles do you think are preventing you from reaching the target condition? And which one are you addressing now? This is an invitation to leaders to serve teams if they can't resolve the obstacle themselves. Coaching Kata is also an invitation to learn as an Agile team and the coach alike. The team is learning about applying scientific thinking and the use of Improvement Kata, and the coach is guiding the team through the cycle and turning this into mutual growth and connection.

Beside the coaching cycle, Agile leaders serve Agile teams by protecting their space for experimentation. Although servant leaders can provide guidance and mentoring based on their experience, they wouldn't judge or rule certain approaches out. Because Agile leaders are commonly not the ones doing the work themselves, it's the Agile team that needs to rally behind the approach taken.

Empowerment and Trust

At the beginning of my career as a software engineer, I had the pleasure of working very closely with a senior manager who was steering a large IT program I was part of. At one point, the topic of trust came up, and I wanted to hear from him how people would gain his trust. His answer was

---

7.   [RG1977]

simple and has guided me well ever since. He said, "I am already trusting everyone here. They have been hired; we trust you by default. You don't have to win my trust."

I noticed that he delegated many responsibilities and decision-making to the team. In hindsight he was probably a very early version of the Agile leaders that organizations are looking for these days.

A culture of trust is key when an organization embraces Agile Kata. When navigating the unknown in complex territory, close to the edge of chaos, team members need to take risks without the fear of blame. It's in the nature of an experiment that it may succeed or fail. Setting a next target condition requires courageous team members. Innovation, not to be confused with invention, is a continuous and incremental effort. The pattern of Agile Kata can create an environment for innovation and scientific thinking, but it requires a trusted environment in which everyone feels comfortable to propose new ideas, contribute, and collaborate effectively during the experiments. Due to the high degree of self-organization and self-management (setting the target condition) in Agile Kata, trust is an important ingredient for success.

Empowerment refers to the process of giving employees the authority to make decisions within their role, including control over resources. In terms of Agile Kata, it means that leaders provide tools, information, and support through servant leadership and motivate employees to take initiative. Although empowered teams typically experience increased motivation as well as improved performance and creativity, these benefits don't come overnight. As with any habit that changes, Agile leaders reinforce their message and live by the values they would like to create over time.

For example, performing Improvement Kata can have significant benefits for Agile (servant) leaders. The pattern helps Agile teams gain a higher level of autonomy through self-setting target conditions and performing experiments. Following the pattern from a leader's perspective creates a higher level of delegation and empowerment.

Ask your product owners whether they can make all budgetary decisions or someone else manages the financials. Or ask your Agile teams if they can purchase and use the tools they need without approval within appropriate guardrails called enabling constraints? If you answer any of these with a no or a maybe, your organization is probably driving with the brakes on. The higher the degree of empowerment, the higher the chances for a successful Agile Kata environment.

Agile Culture

The number one reason why Agile transformations fail is the lack of cultural change.[8] Cultural change is difficult and time-consuming. And by no means do I want to portray that making cultural change is easy simply because you use Agile Kata. The problem with existing methods and

---

8.   McKinsey & Company, "The 5 Trademarks of Agile Organizations."

processes is they often act like a playbook, prescription, or step-by-step guide. Because existing company cultures differ vastly, a one-size-fits-all approach is not a promising idea. There is no universal methodology or framework that can be applied blindly to all situations.

In a traditional command-and-control environment, change is typically introduced top-down. A model or goal is set and then managed like an internal project. From a leadership perspective, it seems easy to dictate cultural change, but this approach is frustrating because it does not stick! That is something that happens in any cultural change and is not specific to Agile.

Transforming to real and long-lasting agility requires a different approach. With Agile Kata, I offer that alternative. By using the direction strategically and being tactical by experimenting daily toward a small target, repetition and deliberate practice of this pattern will make culture stick.

You can quickly explain the pattern, and you can use this book to communicate it. The full power lies in the daily practice and coaching. Not only do Agile leaders give the green light for change, but they are also part of it.

Agile leaders listen carefully to what is happening in the organization, learn from it, and adjust behavior accordingly. They help others through the transition, empathetically connect with people in the organization, and create a safe space for change.

Agile Kata provides a great angle for leaders to connect as they observe and understand the obstacles at hand in a coaching cycle and learning about the progress of a team toward the target condition on a storyboard. Visiting the gemba is also essential. Motivate teams by encouraging more self-organization, and give them the playing field they need.

In addition, Agile leaders live by the Agile principles and collaborate similarly to the way teams do internally. For example, a group of Agile leaders may work with an Agile coach themselves using the Agile Kata to drive initiatives.

Summary

Leaders are part of the transition to Agile; they are not only the sponsors. Part of that change is learning new skills, embodying Agile leadership characteristics, setting goals, and converting to a different leadership style called Agile leadership.

There is a ton to change and learn for leaders in transition. Don't worry; you aren't alone. You can ask an Agile coach for help, ask one to coach you, or ask one to be a mentor or teach you. Bring Agile coaches to your next event or meeting as a facilitator.

Learn for yourself. Experience changes in action by visiting coaching cycles or by being at the gemba. Take baby steps, be patient, and let this Japanese proverb influence your leadership style: "Fall down seven times, stand up eight."[9]

---

9.   [KA2020]

Reflection

- What personal mindset shifts do you need to embrace to lead and support an Agile culture effectively?

- How can you model the Agile principles in your daily actions and decision-making?

- What obstacles and resistance to Agile Kata exist in your organization? How can you proactively address them?

- How can you create a safe environment that encourages experimentation?

- In what ways can you support and develop others in your organization to grow their skills in practicing Agile Kata?

- How could you use Agile Kata for the initiatives in your organization?

- What feedback mechanism could you put into place to gather insights from teams and adapt accordingly?

- Can you name the key success factor for your cultural transformation in your organization, and how can the Agile Kata help you achieve it?

- Do you have a personal bias or assumption that could impact your ability to lead cultural change with Agile Kata?

- What specific actions can you take to create a culture of continuous improvement?

- What are you doing to empower a team or colleagues to self-organize and make decisions independently?

PART III

USE CASES

This book contains three parts, and each part maps to different questions. Part I addressed reasons *why* scientific thinking is so important when we navigate the complicated and complex domains in the Cynefin framework. I also shared reasons Improvement Kata and Coaching Kata make great practice routines to get started with scientific thinking. This is an important, if not essential, skill because technology teams often find themselves in those domains.

Part II covered questions that ask *what*. I explained what Agile Kata is and defined what practices extend the core Improvement and Coaching Kata. Those practices were grouped into topics around collaboration, coaching, leadership, and measuring value. All those practices were anchored around what an Agile mindset is.

In this third and last part of the book, the perspective switches one more time and explores five vastly different use cases to see *how* the Agile Kata can be used among Agile practitioners to address common challenges.

I'm sure you already had some initial ideas about Agile Kata and how you can apply it within your context. I think that is quite normal, but it's also a testament to Kata being a meta-skill. As a universal pattern to increase agility, Agile Kata can touch so many different areas, from a team level to an organizational level.

My goal with this part is not to provide a complete list of use cases but to share five common situations (not case studies) Agile professionals often find themselves in and shine a spotlight on them. These are not cookie cutter recipes. You need to refine your approach depending on the situation you are in. The good news is that Agile Kata can guide you.

The use cases are examples to give you concrete *starting points* to apply Agile Kata. Note the emphasis on *starting point* here. I recognize that the five use cases described are only the tip of the iceberg of what could be presented. Over the years, I saw plenty of teams using Agile Kata for a variety of different things, some being very specific and not necessarily relevant enough for a wider audience. Therefore, I picked five that are common and often used as a theme for improvements. Their scope varies; some cover a small radius and target a single team, whereas others are much wider in radius and can span across departments or the entire organization.

In the beginning of this book, when I talked about the origins of Agile Kata, I mentioned my desire to solve an Agile transformations challenge for my clients. You will find that particular use case repeated here as one of the five use cases. The other four should give you additional ideas on how Agile Kata can be used as a team process to increase business agility or product management.

First is a use case that is useful for any Agile team that runs retrospectives. Because there are hundreds of thousands of Scrum teams around the world, plus other teams that use retrospectives on a regular basis, this use case is truly a bread-and-butter example.

9

Retrospectives

This use case applies to all Agile teams that use a process that includes iterations and retrospectives. This is not only for Scrum teams, but I am using Scrum in this use case to make the example more concrete.

Over the past 25 or so years, the Scrum process framework has changed quite a bit, which is visible in the revision history of the Scrum Guide. Roughly every one or two years, Jeff Sutherland and Ken Schwaber have revised the Scrum Guide. While I was writing this book, the Scrum Guide from November 2020[1] was valid. One event that has been consistently part of the evolution of Scrum was the so-called sprint retrospective, the final event at the end of each sprint. (Sprint is also known as an iteration in other Agile processes, such as Extreme Programming.)

During a sprint retrospective the scrum team inspects how the last sprint went in regard to individuals, interactions, processes, tools, and their definition of done. This scrum event not only serves a scrum team for improving their lives and making their work and time together more enjoyable, but it also gives them opportunities to find ways to increase the quality of their product.[2]

It is very typical that teams can find many ways to improve. The only limiting factor is the time that they dedicate to their retrospective. Therefore, prioritizing the improvement ideas based on their impact plays a big role at the end of that team event.

---

1. https://scrumguides.org/docs/scrumguide/v2020/2020-Scrum-Guide-US.pdf

2. [EDDL2006]

Types of Retrospective Outcomes

Some of the improvement ideas can be done by the team alone. No approval or permission is needed. For example, one team found their work environment cold, dull, and gray and wanted to do something about it. They decided to grow plants. There are certainly situations where you might need approval for growing plants in your office, but not in the example I am referring to. No external help was required to do that. In a case like this when the idea is clear, just do it—no need for Agile Kata.

When the improvement idea is not as straightforward and carries complexity, many scrum teams track the improvement as a to-do item in the sprint backlog of the following sprint. Teams take the improvement item, just like a regular product backlog item, into their next sprint, but one concern is the sprint length. Time-boxing serves teams well for building features and items and planning in two-week intervals. Maybe for you it's one week, three weeks, four weeks, or anything in between. The Scrum Guide states it should be one month or less. The issue is that it's extremely unlikely that an improvement idea will be completed exactly within the sprint boundaries.

Agile Kata as a Parallel Activity to Scrum

Teams practicing time-boxed iterations such as two-week sprints can create a parallel activity to their sprint rhythm that is separated from that product development cadence. Here the storyboard would be visible next to the board of the sprint. During a daily scrum, the team would review both boards. When the sprint ends and the improvement idea is not completed yet, the activity on the storyboard will continue. If the improvement item is resolved earlier, other improvement ideas will get started while the current sprint is in flight. That separation of continuous improvement and a product development rhythm can be helpful.

Then there are improvement ideas that originated from within a team, but the resolution of the improvement must happen outside a team's boundary. Not only is the outcome of the improvement item out of their hands, but the team members would also like to focus on building the product instead of focusing and managing process improvement. Examples include how office space and locations are used or the introduction of new collaboration tools.

Sure, there are certainly teams with a blank check to make these decisions themselves, but, in my experience, most of the times they don't.

In this case, an Agile coach or scrum master assembles a new team, which is valid while the improvement item is pending. The Agile team can keep focusing on building the product while the improvement item becomes a parallel external activity. The scrum master then updates the scrum team during the daily scrum about the progress being made and is transparent using a storyboard. Even better, the improvement team meets right in front of the storyboard in the team area.

Challenges and Opportunities

My experience working with scrum teams is that many teams do not take full advantage of the sprint retrospectives. Some shorten it to something that is less meaningful, and others skip it altogether, unfortunately. Why is it that some scrum teams struggle to initiate continuous improvement when utilizing sprint retrospectives?

The following challenges with retrospectives also provide opportunities for Agile Kata:

- Improvement ideas come in different forms and shapes. There is no cookie cutter way of working.

- Improvement items might be very large, very small, or anywhere in between. Therefore, they might require more time to implement than the sprint length offers.

- If improvement items span across iterations, new items are being identified in the next retrospective, way before the previous one is completed. That demoralizes many in the improvement effort.

- The existing format of the Sprint Backlog artifact may not be suitable for managing the improvement item. For example, physical and electronic tools (scrum boards) are created and streamlined for product backlog items, not to implement improvement ideas about the process itself.

- External members of an improvement team may not be familiar with the Agile process and the vocabulary, but they are important change agents to be involved.

- Teams often remember events that happened shortly before the sprint retrospective more easily than the events that occurred in the beginning of the sprint. That is quite normal for humans, but it does not change the fact that the earlier improvement ideas are less important.

A lack of drive to improve is one of the symptoms of Zombie Scrum behavior.[3] In my experience with new scrum teams, they often start strong in the beginning, but after a few sprints, the retrospective tends to reflect a lack of drive and commitment.

My saddest moments are when I hear scrum teams skip their retrospectives entirely or when developers skip because they don't see any value in them anymore. I am disappointed when I hear, "It won't matter what we discuss; nothing will ever change here," or, "We proposed that idea last time and nobody did anything about it." These are just two examples that indicate the retrospective has lost its life for that team.

Agile Kata can become your companion to break through these problems and energize your improvement efforts again. It becomes a "process" parallel to the existing Agile team process (Figure 9.1). Instead of managing the items on the sprint backlog within the same time box, the Agile Kata storyboard will make the improvement transparent and, therefore, more manageable.

---

3.   [CVJS2020]

Figure 9.1
Agile Kata in parallel to Agile team process

Approach

When there is a parallel improvement process, the team continues with their scrum as-is. Agile Kata can be seen as a supporting process—a spark that stems from the sprint retrospective that ignited the improvement effort. Once Agile Kata has reached its challenge, a new challenge is identified. That creates clarity, transparency, and focus.

Activity: Following Up on Sprint Retrospective Improvement Ideas

- As a scrum master or Agile coach, step back in time and reflect on the improvement ideas from your past two to three sprint retrospectives.

- Check which of the items are still open.

- Meet with the team and quickly order the list of open improvement items.

- Take the highest ranked item and craft a challenge statement that is measurable.

- Find ways to identify the current condition. This might require additional, individual time and might not get completed in the same session.

- Have the scrum team define a small step forward and set the target condition.

- Based on the target condition, define a first experiment as a team on how to get to the target condition.

However, not everybody uses Scrum. You might be applying Kanban or Extreme Programming (XP) as an alternative, and maybe you're scaling with SAFe, to mention some currently popular frameworks and methods. Every team that is using some form of iterative process can follow the same approach. Processes without time-boxing, like the Kanban method, could simply have a retrospective when previous improvement ideas were completed.

Don't forget that retrospectives do not happen only at the end of each sprint or iteration. On a product level, a retrospective might be scheduled after product releases, changes to the team composition, or a major event or milestone.

Reflection

- How likely is it in your team or organization that a team skips the sprint retrospective?

- How valuable are the sprint retrospectives for you?

- If there is one thing you would like to change about your sprint retrospectives, what would it be?

- How likely is it that improvement ideas identified in a sprint retrospective are implemented shortly after?

- How long or short are your sprint retrospectives, and is there enough time to discuss the improvement ideas in sufficient detail?

- What is the range of topics that emerge in your sprint retrospective?

- What is the percentage of improvement ideas that the team can tackle themselves compared to topics for which the team needs organizational support from leaders?

- What is your process for improving how you perform retrospectives?

10

Agile Team Process

The previous use case was all about using Agile Kata as a parallel process to an existing Agile process (for example, Scrum or Extreme Programming) with the goal to follow through the improvement ideas that stemmed from performing retrospectives. In that case, an Agile team would continue building a product using their existing Agile process while a separate improvement team is using Agile Kata.

This second use case still targets single Agile teams but takes a different approach. Instead of using Agile Kata as a parallel process, it becomes the actual team process. Remember that there are two different ways of looking at Agile Kata.

There is Agile Kata to get you started with continuously improving agility through scientific thinking, which you have read about in most of this book so far. The other way of looking at Agile Kata is by using it as a delivery. When I looked at the original Improvement Kata, I found it remarkable that the following simple four-step process is technically all someone needs to collaborate as a team:

1. What is the direction?

2. Where are you now?

3. What is a small step you can take?

4. Experiment to get there.

What would happen if you had a group of people and gave them a goal? They would probably try to understand the goal more by asking questions. Next, they'd maybe reflect on their situation at hand. If the step between the current situation and the goal is too big to take in one single step, they would most likely break it down. Then they might organize themselves to achieve the first step. It is very similar to the way an electrician works or a scientist might approach work in a laboratory.

The difference lies in the domain within the Cynefin framework in which the work exists. If there is a good understanding of the work and goal, current best practices may serve the team well. Think of a compliance review, manufacturing, or installation of a software product in a known environment. The situation may not be 100 percent predictable, but most likely scenarios are expected.

However, knowledge work is different. When there is little to no repetition—for example, building a new product with emerging technology—experimentation is an appropriate way to navigate the unknown and to learn. Throughout this book, you have already learned that Agile Kata is a pattern to explore the learning zone by moving the threshold of knowledge forward. Why not then apply Agile Kata as a team process, especially when the teams are confronted with complicated and complex situations?

Ask a Scrum team about their Agile process, and you most likely hear things like *sprint* (timebox), *product backlog* (artifact), *scrum master* (role), or *daily scrum* (event). These are example elements of a process framework. But you will most likely also hear things like *backlog refinement meeting*, *user stories*, or *estimation*, just to name a few. Those are practices that have emerged over time. Unfortunately, those also become best practices for some teams and are so tightly blended with the framework that it can be difficult to separate them from one another. When that happens, you overhear statements such as, "Every team is using the Fibonacci sequence for estimating," "Everyone has to stand in the daily scrum," or "That's an epic!"

If we are isolating the practices and separate them from the four-step sequence of Agile Kata, would Agile Kata fulfill the definition of an Agile process? Could Agile Kata serve as an alternative to Scrum or Kanban, to name some popular Agile processes?

Let's explore elements and key characteristics of existing Agile processes to see the differences and similarities to Agile Kata.

Timeboxing

Timeboxing has been demonstrated to be an effective approach countless times, especially when transitioning teams from traditional waterfall processes to Agile processes in the early 2000s. It acted as an enabling constraint, creating a new level of urgency, transparency, and opportunities to inspect and adapt, as well as limiting work in progress. The iterations often become the heartbeat of an Agile team. Timeboxing, is of course, not a requirement to be Agile.

As a matter of fact, the Agile Manifesto is silent about timeboxed iterations. The Kanban method is a good example that not every Agile process or method uses iterations.

Many Agile teams use processes that leverage timeboxing, but members began questioning the effectiveness of the approach. Urgency, transparency, and the ability to change are still relevant, of course, but maybe there are other ways to do that. Many professionals share their tips and tricks to work in iterative ways—for example, when estimating or planning work. The goal here is to teach others how to make timeboxing work. For many, it's not natural to think this way. What would happen if we removed the fixed timebox and let teams organize work without it?

Once an iteration is planned and started, it's quite typical that teams are challenged with additional work that impacts the iteration in progress. This is neither intentional nor desired, but it seems to be the new reality. In the early days of Agile processes, when iterations were often three to four weeks long, you could simply shorten the length as a remedy. Nowadays, with one- or two-week iterations being the new norm, there is hardly any buffer left to shorten the iteration further. Of course, you could try to change the situation by teaching and coaching the business, but who is the audience here? Are you trying to change the way your clients want to work with you?

Agile Kata handles timeboxing differently; it's much more casual. Let's say the challenge is to build a new accounting system, and you are just about to start the development effort. Your first target condition could be a capability to manage a basic account type. An Agile team would self-organize, possibly as a mob, and develop toward the target. The team may or may not add a quick reminder on their calendar (achieve-by date) that they will use to revisit the approaches taken when that date is reached. This does not conclude an iteration; it's used as a reflection point about the experiments taken so far. It's not time that creates urgency, but how teams work together on one feature at a time. In many instances, an Agile team will finish the feature before the achieve-by date is even reached. Working this way reduces the chances of being interrupted, because who would interrupt a team that bundles all its energy around one feature? It would be much more natural to line up something to be worked on next, which does not cause any interruptions. The challenge, set by leaders, creates the overarching energy and focus among the team members.

Artifacts

Many teams are using a so-called "product backlog" as an inventory of work that is not done yet. It gives these backlog items a home. Many write them as user stories, something the business would understand and is even able to submit themselves. You might keep that container when using Agile Kata, although I refer to it as a *katalog*, or use something entirely different.

Earlier in this chapter, I mentioned that more and more so-called "best-practices" crept into Agile ways of working, although they aren't Agile or part of a specific framework. Many of them had good intentions but turned out to be problematic in terms of agility. The "definition of ready" is a good example. The engineers I met want to build and release features but don't want to end-lessly talk about the request. Checking whether a request fulfills certain criteria that indicate if it is ready to be worked on does not sound enticing to them. Agile Kata, with its experiment-based approach, can bring back that can-do attitude to Agile processes.

The Agile Kata storyboard is still an artifact, but it's seen more as an artifact to getting started. Revising or removing the storyboard over time is always an option. There is no iteration plan or sprint backlog in Agile Kata.

Roles

The Agile Kata knows only two roles: a team and a coach. Sometimes there is a second coach. The Agile Kata coach is responsible for fostering a culture of scientific thinking and helping the team to become a high-performing Agile team. Agile Kata coaches do not need to uphold a specific process. The goal is to create one with the team that works for them, either from scratch or, if they choose to do so, by starting with an existing process framework. Remember, though, that Agile Kata may be sufficient on its own.

A team in Agile Kata is cross-functional, which means the members have complementary skills set to create a feature. If they lack a skill, they acquire it either through learning or bringing in a person with that skill to the team. Agile Kata does not have predefined roles of a customer or product owner. Depending on the given direction (Step 1 of the Agile Kata pattern), they may add representatives from the business to the team to learn about the domain.

Events

Among scrum teams, the terms *sprint* and *iteration* are often used interchangeably. A sprint has a fixed length, and a team would know how long a sprint would be when they enter it. It's not a rule in Scrum, but the fixed length of a sprint often stays consistent over a longer period of time. The sprint length is nonnegotiable, which creates urgency and focus on value. Sprints are examples of fixed timeboxes. All other events in Scrum are timeboxed too, and they have a maximum number of minutes or hours allotted to them.

There are also non-time-boxed iterations, which are common in science and research. In this case, the focus shifts to completing work, regardless of how long it takes. To prevent this from happening, Agile Kata teams collaborate on a feature, either as a mob or in pairs. They can also place an "achieve-by" date on their storyboard. That is a reminder, not a fixed timebox, for the team to reflect on the current approach. When the achieve-by date is reached, they might decide to continue or stop and reorganize. Providing flexibility and a checkpoint at the same time, which is helpful when teams explore complex situations, is a great combination.

Agile Kata embraces the concept of an iteration, but not a timebox. Because Agile Kata teams don't know exactly how long the iteration will be, planning the time ahead with work does not make sense. Iteration planning, or sprint planning in Scrum, does not exist among Agile Kata teams. And because the sprint goal is replaced by a target condition, a daily scrum becomes unnecessary because team members are already collaborating on a higher frequency than daily. If they recognize a need to hold an event that matches the purpose of a daily scrum, they should certainly do it. This would be a great example of self-organization.

Instead, Agile Kata teams define a state that serves as the next target, and they don't plan the work beyond that first target. They identify an obstacle between the two states and then design and agree on an experiment. Over time, by removing hurdle after hurdle and making more progress, the target condition is eventually reached. The daily coaching cycle is a reflection point for the team to evaluate the target condition, obstacles, and experiment. That is different from a daily scrum.

Each Agile Kata cycle is an iteration (Step 4, "experiment to get there"), and another iteration closes with a retrospective when the next target condition is reached.

Rules

I remember a conversation with a team about the daily scrum. They found this event extremely useful, and it added a lot of value to them. I asked, "Should we try to see what happens if we have it twice a day?" The team was truly surprised by that suggestion because they interpreted the rule as a maximum, whereas I saw it as a minimum. As a result of that conversation, we began an experiment.

If you're thinking about using Agile Kata as your team process, I recommend taking a look at the work of Hirotaka Takeuchi and Ikujiro Nonaka and more specifically the article "The New New Development Game,"[1] which was released in the *Harvard Business Review* in 1986. This article influenced the creation of Scrum and even gave it its name.

There are no references to product owners, scrum masters, or developers in that original article by Takeuchi and Nonoka. You will not find references to the events you are familiar with in Scrum, such as planning, daily scrum, or sprint review. The paper also doesn't provide concrete artifacts like a product backlog, sprint backlog, or increment. I revisited this article and wanted to see whether "The New New Development Game" could have also been an inspiration for the Agile Kata. I found some interesting parallels in how agile teams can structure their team process around the four-step sequence (Figure 10.1).

---

1.   https://hbr.org/1986/01/the-new-new-product-development-game

Figure 10.1
Agile Kata as a team process

Takeuchi and Nonoka identified six characteristics of their so-called holistic method that would fit together like a jigsaw puzzle, as they describe it in their article. Let's take a look at those characteristics to see how Agile Kata connects with them.

- *Built-in instability:* The involvement of top management is to provide the challenge and direction for the Agile Kata team. Top management also creates space and freedom for the teams so that they can aim to meet the sometimes extremely challenging goals.

- *Self-organizing project teams:* Agile Kata teams would operate like a startup company and take initiatives and risks and shape the way they would like to operate. Agile Kata teams show the following conditions: autonomy, self-transcendence, and cross-fertilization.

- *Overlapping development phases:* Agile Kata teams operate as a unit and create rhythm by following the Agile Kata pattern sequence (given challenge, current condition, next target condition, and experimentation). The rhythm in Agile Kata is not created by a timeboxed approach but through the pattern itself.

- *Multilearning:* Through trial and error and experimentation, Agile Kata teams identify promising solutions while narrowing down the list of alternatives through scientific thinking.

- *Subtle control:* Agile Kata teams are not necessarily operating in isolation. Management avoids rigid control that negatively impacts creativity and spontaneity. Subtle control through coaching cycles or go-and-see the actual work (gemba walks) are appropriate tools to prevent a situation from drifting into chaos.

- *Organizational transfer of learning:* Agile Kata teams learn and apply the same scientific thinking across an entire organization, but there is no standardization of processes or so-called best practices. Through coaching and second coaches, organizations multiply learning about Agile Kata and the domain they are in.

The beauty of Agile Kata is that teams shape their process and ways of working. The result will not exactly match what others are doing, but that is intentional. Instead of asking how we can teach or coach our employees to copy what somebody else has done in the past, ask them to take ownership of their own process that works in your environment and situation. The Agile principle "Build projects around motivated individuals. Give them the environment and support they need and trust them to get the job done." is a reminder that this is the Agile approach.

Activity

Your executive leadership learned that Agile Kata is a pattern for continuous improvement and not an Agile team process. Prepare an elevator pitch and argue against that statement by using the 12 principles of the Agile Manifesto.[2]

Summary

Agile Kata may come across as simple or maybe even trivial due to the lack of rules, artifacts, and events. Compared to the origins of other Agile processes and the values and principles of the Agile Manifesto, Agile Kata can be classified as an Agile process alternative.

That lightweight approach could mislead some to believe that it's easy to do. The gained freedom and flexibility that Agile Kata provides puts all elements of a process—tools and practices—on the table for evaluation. Agile Kata requires an increased level of self-organization and skills to collaborate effectively with others. If your team likes rhythm and a set of rules, this particular use case of Agile Kata would not be a good choice. On the flip side, this use case aims to provide an alternative process to agility beyond the existing framework and tools.

Reflection

- If you could change one item in your team process, what would it be and why?

- What would your client or product owner say about your process?

- How do you measure the effectiveness of your team's process?

- What is the process of kicking off a new team (also known as process onboarding) in your organization, and what are ways of improving it?

- In what ways would a person in your organization in the role of an Agile coach (or scrum master) grow by using Agile Kata?

---

2.   https://agilemanifesto.org/principles.html

11

Transformations

The goal of the following backstory is to provide context about Agile transformations and related expectations of them. Even though it is unlikely that you experienced exactly the same situation, you may spot some similarities to your environment.

I remember a question-and-answer session with a leadership team of a potential client in the financial sector in New York. It was right at the time when more and more organizations began thinking about making an Agile transformation—probably sometime around 2015. The main intent of the leadership team was to familiarize themselves with what it meant to have an Agile mindset and determine whether an Agile transformation to achieve that mindset would be a good idea. It was a reasonable request for a company that was hearing Agile success stories more frequently.

This session started off with some basic questions, most of them centered around how to deliver value in short intervals while managing customer expectations. However, it quickly spiraled into very specific concerns, and the questions began hitting me faster and from all different angles. It felt like sitting in a hot seat. The conversation peaked when the head of the project management office (PMO) asked me only a few minutes into the meeting, "Joe, I need to know how long a project will take and how much it will cost before I approve it. Can Agile teams provide that answer for me? Yes or no?" After that question, the room fell silent quickly. She then added, "My PMO approves or declines project requests based on that information. It is important for me to know."

All eyes were on me now because the answer to that question seemed to be a concern to everyone in the room. I knew the question would require much more than a yes or no, but I decided to answer with a simple "no." The head of the PMO then replied, "Well, Agile won't be a good fit for us then."

I got the impression that the meeting was about to come to an end. To keep the conversation going, I wanted to know if I could inject a question. The leadership team, which seemed to have moved on already, replied, "Sure, what would you like to know?" I wanted to know how they were doing with estimating time and costs. "Terrible!" was the answer from the head of the PMO. She then reminded me that this was the reason why they brought me in. They wanted to see if Agile ways of working would fix their existing PMO issue. She immediately mentioned that she wasn't interested in transforming her organization to Agile if the problem of estimating time and costs would continue to exist.

I wanted to know what "terrible" meant, and she began filling me in on a company secret. "Every time a team submits an estimate, I double the estimate behind the scenes," she said, before continuing with a smile, "because software engineers are highly optimistic." When asked, how many of the projects in her organization were on time, everyone in the room—not only the head of the PMO—replied in unison, "Never!" It appeared to be a running joke among them.

I knew we were getting closer to the pain point in our conversation and the meeting. I also had this feeling that if I asked the team members about their experience estimating, I would be hearing even more frustrations.

At that point in time in the meeting, I felt it was time for me to make a counteroffer and share a new perspective on project management. Beside talking about the existing process, which was obviously not very effective, I wanted to show them what an Agile process could do for them. So far, their arguments were related to making a process fit their existing rules. They never asked what rules need to change to make Agile work. It requires a cultural change; their existing approval process was a piece of their company culture.

I started off by saying that "Agile teams are never late." It got quiet in the room again, and it seemed that everyone was processing that statement carefully. One of the leaders asked, "How can you say that?" A few leaders, who had been about to leave the room, took a seat again. The statement seemed to raise interest among the participants, and the meeting continued.

To answer the question, I began talking about increments, definition of *done*, cross-functionally organized teams, and so forth. I mentioned that by the end of an iteration, an Agile team has something that is potentially shippable. With that discipline in place, a deadline isn't so much of a concern for an Agile team. One of the leaders interrupted to ask, "But if I understand this correctly, we won't know what we are going to ship at the due date, right?"

I replied, "That is correct, but that is a business decision." I explained that the commitment of the Agile teams is to focus on what is most valuable for the business at a given point in time. However, representatives from the business need to be in a dialogue with the Agile teams throughout—not only in the very early stages of a project but to the very end. I began to earn support among the participants. Body language and tone had changed compared to the beginning of the meeting. The leaders agreed with each other on some fundamentals and began nodding.

Instead of big bang waterfall efforts overseen by a PMO, which often had an "us versus them" attitude, we were beginning to design a potential partnership between the business and IT directly. I also offered that an Agile team could revisit the product roadmap at meaningful intervals—let's say every three months—and gave them an exit strategy when things didn't work out the way they anticipated. They'd be able to stop the project early. Even in this case, they could still use what they had created so far. By being fixated on addressing one concern (PMO predictions of delivery dates), they never saw the other potential benefits they would have missed.

By the end of the meeting, which was almost cut short in the beginning, we had a meaningful conversation about goals and direction for the organization. As a result, they decided to start their Agile transformation.

The Continuous Improvement Approach

The client meeting I described was one of the many triggers that made me think about the Agile transformation process. Back then, Agile Kata did not exist yet, but it began shaping the question, "How can we transform an organization to Agile in Agile ways?" In other words, how can you use an Agile approach to an Agile transformation? Today, I would certainly introduce Agile Kata as that response.

A dictionary definition of the word *transformation* could be a change in form, appearance, nature, or character. The conversion of caterpillar into a butterfly is a transformation. That kind of transformation is final. The butterfly stays to the very end of life as a butterfly. It doesn't revert back to being a caterpillar or change into something else.

Agile transformations, on the other hand, are continuous. The Agile Manifesto even starts with the words, "We are uncovering better ways," which emphasizes that Agile requires an ongoing curious mindset that includes the desire to increase agility beyond what we know today.

Every time clients ask me when the Agile transformation would "end," I let them know that it could come to an end anytime, but that would imply that they'd stopped improving. Who wants that? In a rapidly changing business world, standing still means going backward. It's like putting money into a zero-interest savings account. Inflation will eat up your wealth over time. Therefore, you can see an Agile transformation as an investment into your company's future, enabling you to react to changing market conditions and innovation. That is a key take-away. Because Agile transformations are continuous and highly complex by nature, they can't be run as a project themselves. In my earlier client example, a transition from a project to a product mindset was needed while introducing Agile processes among teams and leaders, including the PMO.

When an organization has this aha moment to initiate an Agile transformation, those initiatives and aspirations are typically grandiose. It's good to have big ideas and challenges, but they need to be broken down into something manageable. Because there are so many unknowns to navigate, it's impossible to predict the unforeseen. It's like a ship aiming to cross the Atlantic from Europe and predicting a smooth ride to North America because the water at the point of origin is very calm.

The mindset of an Agile transformation must change from a one-time effort with a clear end-date and fixed budget to a continuous Agile change management process (Figure 11.1). As a result, the employees participating in a piece of the Agile transformation need to learn and deliberately practice the Agile Kata pattern. Of course, it's important for everyone to learn how to work in Agile ways when an Agile transformation has begun. However, it's more important to start with the basic pattern of Agile Kata that will drive the Agile transformation. It is the Agile Kata that will give the transformation the direction and cultural change in many small bites.

The sequence and vocabulary of the Agile Kata are easy to memorize. Eventually scientific thinking and Agile Kata will take over. Questions about the target condition, current condition, or experiments will have a brand-new meaning for everyone involved. The reality of Agile transformation processes is unfortunately that many of them are not very Agile themselves.

Figure 11.1
Continuous improvement for Agile transformations

There are two common questions I frequently hear about Agile transformations:

- How do you start an Agile transformation?
- What is the process for the Agile transformation itself?

Let's look at these questions next.

Getting Started

What drew my initial attention to Kata was the fact that its pattern can start at any given moment. It does not have a defined starting point. That is particularly important for an Agile transformation because so many organizations have made initial steps and investments. There is no need to reverse direction. You're still going forward, but in a different way.

With Agile Kata, your initial investment into an Agile transformation isn't a sunk cost. Step 2, "Grasp your current condition," is that starting point. It's a flexible way of picking up the work where you left it off. If you feel that your initial Agile transformation didn't deliver the results you had hoped for, Agile Kata is ready whenever you are ready.

The Process of Transforming

When you replace the plan-driven transformation approach with a pattern approach that enables continuous improvement, you foster a culture of experimentation. Because of that, you won't know exactly what will happen next, but you'll enter the learning zone. The only thing you'll know is that the ideas come from the people closest to the work.

The result of an Agile Kata–enabled culture differs significantly compared to a top-down plan-driven transformation. One common characteristic of a plan-driven transformation is process conformity when people announce, "All of our teams are using ____" (fill in your Agile process of choice). With Agile Kata, teams typically show a higher degree of process diversity, combining many different tools and practices.

You can target a small area of an organization and start there. Inspect and adapt. You can start in multiple corners of the organization with different Agile Kata, which provides a simple way of communicating. The steps are logical: setting a goal, identifying where you are, creating a small step forward, and running experiments to get there. The steps are easy to understand and provide orientation and transparency.

As an alternative to using the four steps, you can instead ask four commonsense questions:

- Where do you want to be?
- Where are you now?
- What is a small step you can take toward your goal?
- What can you try to get there?

This way, you can ask the questions without needing to teach or explain Agile Kata in great detail initially. It is a thinking pattern—not a methodology. This is scientific thinking in action.

Using "Agile transformation" as Step 1, understand the direction or challenge, would be too big of a challenge because it's a moving target. I view this more like the vision.

There's one thing to keep in mind with transformation: You are not in the business of transforming. You are in business to provide value to your clients. I assume you want to utilize agility to improve the way you are doing business.

Maybe you want to use agility to react to market changes better. Maybe you want to explore new markets. Whatever your reasons, I recommend tying your business goals to your Agile transformation goals. They're not separate anymore. The purpose of the transformation is to achieve your business goals more effectively—not to become an expert in a specific and detailed transformation process!

Reflection

- How did the leaders in your organization support your Agile transformation?
- What specific business goals have you achieved as a result of your Agile transformation?
- How effectively are your feedback loops and retrospectives working in driving continuous improvement?
- Can you describe the long-term vision of your Agile transformation?
- How do you measure and define success of your Agile transformation?
- What cultural changes have you observed since the start of your Agile transformation?

12

Business Agility

Business agility is an organization's ability to adapt, respond, and pivot in a rapidly changing business environment. It's often wrongly understood to refer to applying an Agile process within a business unit outside of IT. An Agile process can certainly bring benefits for a marketing or finance team using Scrum or Kanban, and it may mean that the teams within certain departments are becoming more effective. However, the overall business may not necessarily react more quickly to emerging events or market changes as a result. Business agility requires an integration of internal processes, policies, and rules that may span across various departments. Business agility widens the scope of agility from the team level to the enterprise level. Agile processes at a team level are therefore important enablers for business agility, but the sum of all teams being Agile does not equal business agility. Business agility means how the organization as a whole responds to changes and is typically not a team alone, unless a single team is the entire organization. This use case is more relevant for larger organizations and how they can apply Agile Kata to help make their organization react better to external triggers.

When executives talk about business agility, they often see it as meaning they have a lean and nimble organization; their view isn't based on the definition of Agile. From an executive viewpoint, business agility can be achieved without teams working in Agile ways. Agile Kata coaches need to be aware of that distinction and set expectations right before any improvement can begin.

Apart from embracing change, business agility includes the ability and capacity to innovate and effectively adjust structures and processes. With a higher degree of business agility, an organization is more resilient and recognizes opportunities for mitigating risks more effectively. To achieve business agility, Steven J. Spear recommends creating an organizational culture that embraces decentralized decision-making, rapid learning and problem-solving, and continuous improvement.[1]

Think of a company that was founded several years ago around a great idea for a new product. Let's say the product was very successful, demand increased, and the company grew accordingly. New locations and offices were added, as were new employees. Over time, the organizational structure became more complicated, and communication channels slowed down. Quick decisions and reaction time comparable to what the company experienced during the initial years are now no longer possible. Many executives wish they had the rapid response times they enjoyed as a young organization. The issues that stem from growing into a larger organization weren't on anybody's radar because the product was great. Orders kept coming in and were fulfilled. Even though the company's growth might be slowing over time, things are fine, and habits of doing business in a certain way are well established.

Things are fine, that is, until a significant impact hits the company and requires a swift response. In recent years, we have seen this in the music industry, and industries such as publishing, automobile manufacturing, and sales, to name a few. The problem is that the company hadn't prepared for a situation like that. The organization is confronted with change, but it hasn't practiced *how* to change. Without deliberately practicing change, why would the company expect to be good at rapidly changing when the situation requires it? The organizational fitness is considered to be low. The existing org chart probably tells a story of top-down decision-making with command-and-control management. What worked well in the beginning of the business has become a curse.

How can Agile Kata help increase business agility and address this common challenge?

The first order of business is to gain a shared understanding to switching from a reactive approach to a proactive approach. Just like physical fitness, the impact of improving business agility is not something you notice overnight (Figure 12.1). Eating one apple per year the night before your annual physical does not move the needle on your health. *Proactive* means preparing for any future threat you can anticipate, rather than a specific problem that has already materialized. Mitigate risks; don't firefight issues.

---

1.   [SS2010]

Figure 12.1
Continuous improvement to strengthen organizational fitness

If you're facing a situation that requires an immediate reaction, Agile Kata can help you with creating the focus through a disciplined approach. However, if you find yourself in the chaos domain of the Cynefin framework, you will require a swift direct response first. Command and control is the order of the day here. Act, sense, and respond. Going into analysis mode and identifying business agility opportunities is not going to be effective in chaos.

The company in the earlier example is not experiencing an immediate threat, but the leadership signaled that they are all in agreement that they want to revisit the current state of business agility and prepare their organization proactively for the future. They agreed on Agile Kata because of its strong focus on continuous improvement and an Agile mindset. They performed a multiday Open Space event to identify bottlenecks in the current operating model, which were ranked based on customer impact to create a top 10 list. The leadership could decide to tackle multiple bottlenecks in parallel, especially if they are in different parts of the organization, but for the purpose of this use case, I'm sticking with only one.

The bottleneck in the example is the onboarding of new team members for Agile teams, either as independent contractors or full-time employees. That request came from the IT group, where Agile teams are often on the lookout for more talent to build product features. From a business agility perspective, the delay of staffing has a causal connection to the ability to build client features. The issue became clearer and more pressing once more evidence was collected about the existing process.

HR traditionally performed the entire process from start to finish but had many interactions with IT throughout. The back and forth slowed down the process a lot. Then an Agile Kata team, formed around IT, HR professionals, and Agile coaches, kicked off Agile Kata to address that challenge. Analysis of the current condition brought to surface that the onboarding process for new employees took an average of nine weeks and three days. For independent contractors, the time was just under four weeks. A challenge (Step 1) was identified to reduce the onboarding time by 50 percent for both full-time employees and contractors.

Further analysis revealed that getting the job opening posted was a very slow process. There were massive delays caused by back-and-forth communication between HR and IT while HR tried to understand the full needs and asks. Through several small targets and lots of experimentations, there was enough evidence to reduce the interaction between HR and IT. One approach was to delegate the entire job opening and interview process to the hiring department—in this case the IT organization. Once their decision to make an offer and initiate a contract was finalized, it became the first time HR engaged with the candidate. Once both parties agreed and made it official, the hiring department continued with the onboarding of the candidate directly. Every time a person was hired, the effectiveness of the approach was measured, the overall results verified, and further improvements integrated.

For vendors, the IT organization would start owning the relationship with contractors, as well as the agencies and recruiters. This could also lead to an improved process around master service agreements that could then enable even faster onboarding of contractors.

This example shows signs of increased business agility. A higher degree of decentralized decision-making, empowered Agile teams, and more transparency are all signs of improved business agility.

Of course, you can take what was learned from this example and apply it to other contexts to experience significant improvements. Here are some other contexts I could have used to illustrate the impact of improved business agility:

- Procurement
- Finance
- Legal
- Product portfolio

At this point, you might get really excited about improving business agility with Agile Kata, and I applaud that. However, I'm really sorry that I have to hit the brakes because I want to be realistic and manage expectations properly. Any of these improvements leads to long-term change initiatives. Words like *endurance*, *stamina*, and *grit* come to my mind. A company needs to be tough on itself to undergo this type of transformation and be relentless in its actions. It will require ongoing support from leaders and staying focused on the long-term improvement goal while being disciplined about using Agile Kata.

Reflection

- What business threat is your company facing? Can you name a concrete action to mitigate that threat?

- How transparent are your processes?

- What is the current state or condition of the technology in your company?

- Do you have mechanisms in place for continuous learning and knowledge sharing across departments?

- How would you assess the adaptability of your organizational culture?

- Can you think of one example of how decision-making within a team can be improved?

13

Product Management

The use case in Chapter 10 illustrated how Agile Kata can be used as an Agile team process. You saw that Agile Kata can enable teams to work in Agile ways, just as teams work with other existing frameworks and processes, because the pattern of Agile Kata embodies the Agile values and principles.

Building a product is certainly one important step in a product's entire lifecycle, but it's not the only one. Using Scrum as an example, the work of a team often starts with an initial product backlog. Agile teams often receive that product backlog that contains features that are ordered by a product owner. The team then walks over the list of requests in sprints and turns them around as working software. At any time in the process, but especially when teams close the feedback loop with stakeholders, the product backlog is updated. The process is iterative and continuous until the product owner decides to stop.

Where do these product backlog items come from? Do they just emerge magically out of the blue? Of course not. There is typically a product management process that started way before an Agile team begins implementing any features and continues way beyond the delivery of the product. A product management life cycle lasts from inception of the product to the final retirement (also known as *sunsetting*) of the product and is therefore also in motion while an Agile team is building the product.

This risk is that a team might feel that they are operating in isolation. The pipeline of requests often fills up faster than they can be turned around, and the work becomes mechanical like a feature factory. Melissa Perri calls this the "build trap."[1] One reason a team may fall into the build trap is that developers assume that the necessary due diligence took place before items entered the product backlog. Alas, as we know, that is not always the case because the product backlog is always open to new ideas. Everybody can potentially add anything to the product backlog, but not everything is valuable or important. Weeding out the requests that do not have any potential is a crucial activity for the product owner. This is a great flexible concept and an important rule, and I don't want to see that change.

That said, the product owner is a role, not a job description. Being a product owner according to Scrum is by far not everything a typical product manager needs to know and do. Just like the start-to-end product management process, the role of a product owner is a subset of the many accountabilities and responsibilities of a product manager (Figure 13.1).

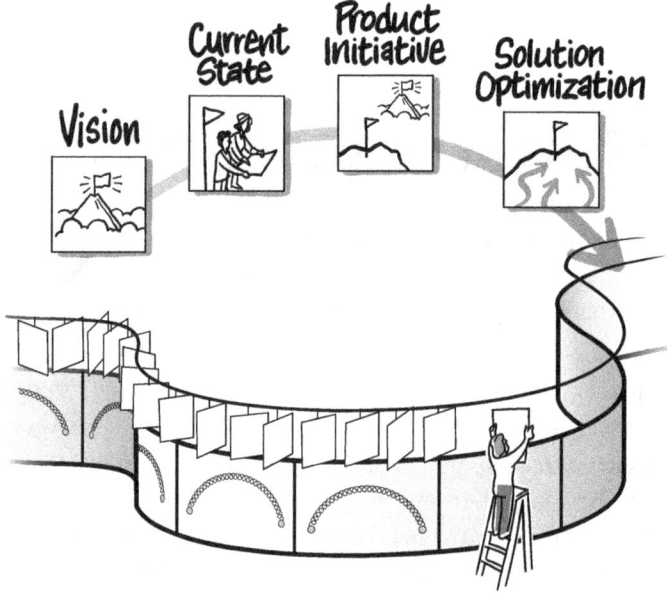

Figure 13.1
Agile Kata as a product management process

Many Scrum teams are asking about good ways of populating a product backlog. Where do these requests come from? What are the criteria for ordering and reordering a product backlog? What is the vision of the product? Who is the potential target audience of the product, and what are they aiming to do with the product? Are there competitive products? How are they positioned? What is a viable price point for the product offering? What does the product launch look like? What is the process for decision-making about conflicting product features raised by different stakeholders? None of these questions are answered by an existing Agile team process

---

1.   [MP2018]

because not every product is being built the same way. That is why the Agile team processes are often frameworks. It is important to emphasize that product managers wear many hats, not only the one of a product owner in Scrum.

Different product management processes are available for different industry and target users. For example, lean start-up[2] uses rapid iterations and learning toward a minimum viable product (MVP). Design thinking[3] is another popular approach that is built around empathy to identify the customer needs. Products that are targeting a highly regulated market often embrace a more controlled Stage Gate process, such as in a pharmaceutical or manufacturing domain where compliance with legal standards is important. More recently, product managers have been looking at the product operating model[4] as a start-to-end product management process. The processes have a focus on product development, not necessarily agility. You might encounter some elements like gates and phases that feel unnatural for an Agile organization. If you're trying to improve business agility as discussed in Chapter 12, you might need to take a closer look at the product management processes as well.

Product managers also have many practices in their toolboxes. Those are not full product development processes but techniques that can be easily integrated with those processes. Lean UX[5] comes to mind. It goes deep on user interface design and user interaction and integrates well with lean start-up and Agile development. Product road mapping and the double diamond problem-solving framework are other examples of practices that can be integrated.

Doesn't that all sound very familiar compared to the examples and situations I covered throughout this book? And just like before, I see two major opportunities for how Agile Kata can be integrated in the product management world: applying Agile Kata as a product management process and a meta-skill to create your own product management process.

Melissa Perri came across Improvement Kata and Coaching Kata by Mike Rother and realized that this pattern was what she had been doing, but she hadn't "kata-fied"[6] it yet. She later called it *Product Kata* and used it as a scientific and systematic way to build better products with her clients. She adjusted the names of the four steps to work with her product management:

- Step 1: Vision and strategic intent

- Step 2: Current state of intents

- Step 3: Product initiative

- Step 4: Problem exploration, solution exploration, and solution optimization

---

2. [ER2011]

3. [TK2001]

4. [MC2024]

5. [JGJS2021]

6. *Agile.FM,* episode 139

If you are using Agile Kata in this way, you apply scientific thinking to the product you're creating. That includes gathering results and evidence that is eventually being evaluated against the product vision. That research could then influence the decisions by a product manager acting out the role of product owner with a Scrum team. Kata builds an important connection between an existing product management process and an Agile team process.

When applying Agile Kata in product management, you manage your product in an Agile way. Agile Kata could therefore be used by a product management organization as a lightweight Agile product management process that feeds the results into a product backlog. Those items might then be pulled by an Agile Kata team that also uses Agile Kata, but as their team process. Agile Kata can scale across different disciplines and scale to a multiteam development effort.

If you're looking for a starting point for a product management process, you will find some references in the back of the book. The focus of this chapter was to give you some ideas on how to incorporate Agile Kata and scientific thinking in your product management organization.

And that is how I would like to close this final chapter of Part III. Agile Kata can be your skill to create your own or fine-tune your existing product management process. By doing so, you are shaping a process that works for you and with agility in mind. Agile Kata is a meta-skill.

Reflection

- How is your product roadmap connected with the Agile development process?

- How do you incorporate customer feedback about increments into your product development process?

- What is your process to delete items from your product backlog?

- What steps are you taking to inspect and adapt the product management process?

- How effectively are you using data and analytics to inform your product decisions?

- How do you measure product success?

- What are the biggest obstacles preventing you from delivering on your product vision?

Wrap-Up

My goal for this book was to shine a spotlight on Agile Kata as a pattern for practicing continuous improvement and scientific thinking. I wanted to share my experiences and insights into the many unique opportunities of Agile Kata. You got to know some of them and how Agile Kata can be used at the different levels of application. I am excited by how Agile Kata can be a benefit at the team or organizational level because it is a universal pattern for increasing agility.

You got to know Agile Kata as a skill-building pattern and as a process-pattern. These two sides of application show the abundance of possible use cases. Many of these common use cases score high with students when I teach Agile Kata courses. I chose five use cases to share in this book and offered several personal stories throughout the book to connect the topics of Agile with kata. From time to time, I also learn from course participants about their own niche use cases that they are planning to use Agile Kata for. Many of those are very specific to a single company. That's OK; I welcome those stories, too. All my conversations with practitioners make me confident that you will identify your own use cases as well.

You can't expect that a book that teaches continuous improvement and learning will bring closure to an entire topic. I see this book more like a starting point. The learning zone is always ahead of you, and there is never a situation where you know everything already, at least not in the complex world we live in. The only way of getting closer to the threshold of knowledge and exploring the unknown is by making a step. Which direction you will take and what your first next step will be is entirely up to you.

My hope is not only that you gained confidence in Agile Kata by reading the book but that you actually try it! Practice does not make perfect; practice makes permanent. I invite you to experiment with Agile Kata, find a use case, practice it, and begin making scientific thinking more permanent.

I don't have a crystal ball, but I do want to take a risk and look further ahead, way beyond my threshold of knowledge. It appears that the current trends in the IT industry require more continuous improvement rather than less. To do that in ways to create more business agility, breaking away from old habits, why not tackle them with Agile Kata? In return, those trends will most likely impact Agile Kata as well.

Generative AI is a good example. On one hand, organizations are looking for ways to transform their organization to use GenAI effectively. Current experiments include self-managed systems and AI-supported operational processes that optimize themselves. To introduce GenAI using agility, Agile Kata could possibly help those looking for a continuous improvement pattern.

On the other hand, GenAI can impact Agile Kata, too. With more and more knowledge and context, a team or an Agile coach can have a permanent partner to bounce new ideas off of. For example, I asked ChatGPT to be my Agile Kata coach, and it was able to perform a coaching cycle with me. I was also able to submit my storyboard as a photo, and ChatGPT was able to analyze it for me. If you are not already as impressed as I was, the photo was of a handwritten document!

There are still issues with AI, of course—ethically and in how it interprets the information about agility it's given—but there is a lot happening in a short period of time. Being prepared for that revolution and how your competition will approach it will test your company's current state of business agility.

Knowledge workers are working in hybrid workspaces more and more often. Those require a digital workspace to enable self-organized teams and agility, but workers also need proper digital tools to perform scientific thinking in teams.

Sustainability, or green IT, is on the rise as well. How green is your IT organization in terms of processing power, e-waste, and data centers? I know this is totally taken out of context, but one Agile principle starts with "Agile processes promote sustainable development." Maybe future Agile Kata teams include eco-related concerns in their decision-making, challenges, target conditions, and experiments. In addition to Agile, green and sustainable development might be another priority when applying Agile Kata in the future.

Quantum computing is a hot topic. Although still in its infancy, the prospect of the sheer processing power could revolutionize complex problem-solving and experimentation. If quantum computing breaks through to a commercial level, the wheel of innovation will spin even faster.

Last but not least is an example that impacts the social structures of software development. The rise of low-code and no-code development platforms for automating businesses is in the hands of many, if not all. More competition and possible solutions may increase the speed of innovation, liberating the many ideas that exist but didn't have access to the technologies yet.

Never ever has business and organizational agility been more important for reacting to changes. I hope I'm leaving you with food for thought, not a sense of overwhelm. I use the examples I've offered to highlight that change is continuous rather than an occasional initiative. Never before has real agility been more important than today, and I'm excited to find out what the future holds.

I hope the spark of Agile Kata has jumped to you.

Bibliography

The following books were either referenced throughout the book, or they are recommended books to continue your learning journey.

[AG1995] Andrew S. Grove, *High Output Management* (New York: Vintage Books, 1995).

[ARMF2020] Dr. Anne Rød and Marita Fridjhon, *Creating Intelligent Teams: Leading with Relationship Systems* (Randburg, Republic of South Africa: KR Publishing, 2020).

[BG2022] Bob Galen, *Extraordinarily Badass Agile Coaching: The Journey from Beginner to Mastery and Beyond* (self-pub, 2022).

[CA1979] Christopher Alexander, *The Timeless Way of Building* (Oxford: Oxford University Press, 1979).

[CVJS2020] Christiaan Verwijs, Johannes Schartau, and Barry Overeem, *Zombie Scrum Survival Guide: A Journey to Recovery* (Boston: Addison-Wesley, 2021).

[CW2021] Christina Wodtke, *Radical Focus: Achieving Your Most Important Goals with Objectives and Key Results*, Second Edition (n.p.: Cucina Media, 2021).

[DK2011] Daniel Kahneman, *Thinking, Fast and Slow* (New York: Farrar, Straus and Giroux, 2013).

[DS2022] Dave Snowden, *Cynefin: Weaving Sense-Making into the Fabric of Our World* (Singapore: Cynefin, 2022).

[DTAH1999] Dave Thomas and Andrew Hunt, *The Pragmatic Programmer: Your Journey to Mastery*, 20th Anniversary Edition, Second Edition (Boston: Addison-Wesley, 2000).

[EDDL2006] Esther Derby and Diana Larsen, *Agile Retrospectives: Making Good Teams Great*, First Edition (Raleigh, NC: Pragmatic Bookshelf, 2006).

[ELJLTR2023] Eduardo Lander, Jeffrey Liker, and Tom Root, *Engaging the Team at Zingerman's Mail Order: A Toyota Kata Comic* (New York: Productivity Press, 2023).

[ER2011] Eric Ries, *The Lean Startup: How Today's Entrepreneurs Use Continuous Innovation to Create Radically Successful Businesses* (New York: Crown Currency, 2011).

[GHJV1994] Erich Gamma, Richard Helm, Ralph Johnson, and John Vlissides, *Design Patterns: Elements of Reusable Object-Oriented Software* (Boston: Addison-Wesley, 1995).

[GW2005] Gerald Weinberg, *Weinberg on Writing: The Fieldstone Method* (New York: Dorset House, 2005).

[HLKC2014] Henri Lipmanowicz and Keith McCandless, *The Surprising Power of Liberating Structures: Simple Rules to Unleash a Culture of Innovation* (self-pub, 2014).

[HH2020] Heidi Helfand, *Dynamic Reteaming: The Art & Wisdom of Changing Teams*, Second Edition (Sebastopol, CA: O'Reilly, 2020).

[HO2008] Harrison Owen, *Open Space Technology: A User's Guide*, Third Edition (Oakland, CA: Berrett-Koehler, 2008).

[JA2010] Jurgen Appelo, *Management 3.0: Leading Agile Developers, Developing Agile Leaders* (Boston: Addison-Wesley, 2011).

[JA2012] Jurgen Appelo, *How to Change the World: Change Management 3.0* (self-pub, 2012).

[JC2018] James Clear, *Atomic Habits: An Easy & Proven Way to Build Good Habits & Break Bad Ones* (New York: Avery, 2018).

[JCJP2011] Jim Collins and Jerry I. Porras, *Built to Last: Successful Habits of Visionary Companies*, Third Edition (New York: Harper Collins, 2011).

[JD2018] John Doerr, *Measure What Matters: How Google, Bono, and the Gates Foundation Rock the Works with OKRs*, Second Edition (Northwood, UK: Portfolio, 2018).

[JEJB2020] Jutta Eckstein and John Buck, *Company-Wide Agility with Beyond Budgeting, Open Space & Sociocracy: Survive & Thrive on Disruption* (self-pub, 2020).

[JGJS2021] Jeff Gothelf and Josh Seiden, *Lean UX: Designing Great Products with Agile Teams*, Third Edition (Sebastopol, CA: O'Reilly, 2021).

[JGJS2024] Jeff Gothelf and Josh Seiden, *Who Does What by How Much?: A Practical Guide to Customer-Centric OKRs* (Brooklyn, NY: 2024).

[JH1999] Jim Highsmith, *Adaptive Software Development: A collaborative Approach to Managing Complex Systems* (New York: Dorset House, 2000).

[JH2023] Jim Highsmith, *Wild West to Agile: Adventures in Software Development Evolution and Revolution* (Boston: Addison-Wesley, 2023).

[JK2023] Joshua Kerievsky, *Joy of Agility: How to Solve Problems and Succeed Sooner* (Dallas, TX: Matt Holt, 2023).

[JL2020] Jeffrey Liker, *The Toyota Way: 14 Management Principles from the World's Greatest Manufacturer*, Second Edition (New York: McGraw Hill, 2020).

[JSJJ] Jeff Sutherland and J. J. Sutherland, *Scrum: The Art of Doing Twice the Work in Half the Time* (New York: Crown Currency, 2014).

[JTLH2024] Jason Tanner and Luke Hohmann, *Software Profit Streams: A Guide to Designing a Sustainably Profitable Business* (self-pub, 2024).

[JPTS2020] Jonathan Passmore and Tracy Sinclair, *Becoming a Coach: The Essential ICF Guide* (Princeton, NJ: Springer, 2020).

[JKHR2016] John Kotter and Holger Rathgeber, *Our Iceberg Is Melting: Changing and Succeeding Under Any Conditions* (New York: Penguin Random House, 2016).

[JT2006] Jean Tabaka, *Collaboration Explained: Facilitation Skills for Software Project Leaders* (Boston: Addison-Wesley, 2006).

[JTNTBR2020] John Turner, Nigel Thurlow, and Brian Rivera, *The Flow System: The Evolution of Agile and Lean Thinking in an Age of Complexity* (Dallas, TX: 3 Helix Publishing, 2020).

[JTNT2023] John Turner and Nigel Thurlow, *The Flow System Playbook* (Dallas, TX: 3 Helix Publishing, 2023).

[JW2024] John Willis, *Deming's Journey to Profound Knowledge: How Deming Helped Win a War, Altered the Face of Industry, and Holds the Key to Our Future* (Portland, OR: IT Revolution Press, 2024).

[KA2020] Katie Anderson, *Learning to Lead, Leading to Learn: Lessons from Toyota Leader Isao Yoshino on a Lifetime of Continuous Learning* (San Francisco: Integrand LLC, 2020).

[KLSK2024] Klaus Leopold and Siegfried Kaltenecker, *Flight Levels: Leading Organizations with Business Agility* (self-pub, 2024).

[KMBR2023] Patricia Kong, Todd Miller, Kurt Bittner, and Ryan Ripley, *Unlocking Business Agility with Evidence-Based Management: Satisfy Customers and Improve Organizational Effectiveness* (Boston: Addison-Wesley, 2024).

[KSMB2001] Ken Schwaber and Mike Beedle, *Agile Software Development with Scrum* (Upper Saddle River, NJ: Pearson, 2002).

[LA2010] Lyssa Adkins, *Coaching Agile Teams: A Companion for Scrum Masters, Agile Coaches, and Project Managers in Transition* (Boston: Addison-Wesley, 2010).

[LCJG2009] Lisa Crispin and Janet Gregory, *Agile Testing: A Practical Guide for Testers and Agile Teams* (Boston: Addison-Wesley, 2009).

[LCJG2014] Lisa Crispin and Janet Gregory, *More Agile Testing: Learning Journeys for the Whole Team* (Boston: Addison-Wesley, 2015).

[MBCC1999] Marcus Buckingham and Curt Coffman, *First, Break All the Rules: What the World's Greatest Managers Do* (New York: Gallup Press, 1999).

[MC2024] Marty Cagan, *Transformed: Moving to the Product Operating Model* (Hoboken, NJ: Wiley, 2024).

[MMLR2004] Mary Lynn Manns and Linda Rising, *Fearless Change: Patterns for Introducing New Ideas* (Boston: Addison-Wesley, 2005).

[MMLR2015] Mary Lynn Manns and Linda Rising, *More Fearless Change: Strategies for Making Your Ideas Happen* (Boston: Addison-Wesley, 2015).

[MP2018] Melissa Perri, *Escaping the Build Trap: How Effective Product Management Creates Real Value* (Sebastopol, CA: O'Reilly, 2018).

[MPDT2023] Melissa Perri and Denise Tilles, *Product Operations: How Successful Companies Build Better Products at Scale* (New York: Product Institute, 2023).

[MPTP2003] Mary Poppendieck and Tom Poppendieck, *Lean Software Development: An Agile Toolkit* (Boston: Addison-Wesley, 2003).

[MR2009] Mike Rose, *Writer's Block: The Cognitive Dimension* (Carbondale, IL: Southern Illinois University Press, 2009).

[MR2018] Mike Rother, *The Toyota Kata Practice Guide: Practicing Scientific Thinking Skills for Superior Results in 20 Minutes a Day* (New York: McGraw Hill, 2018).

[MR2009] Mike Rother, *Toyota Kata: Managing People for Improvement, Adaptiveness, and Superior Results* (New York: McGraw Hill, 2009).

[MRJS1999] Mike Rother and John Shook, *Learning to See: Value Stream Mapping to Add Value and Eliminate MUDA* (Boston: Lean Enterprise Institute, 1999).

[MSMP2019] Matthew Skelton and Manuel Pais, *Team Topologies: Organizing Business and Technology Teams for Fast Flow* (Portland, OR: IT Revolution Press, 2019).

[PP2020] Priya Parker, *The Art of Gathering: How We Meet and Why It Matters* (Riverhead, NY: Riverhead Books, 2020).

[RG1977] Robert K. Greenleaf, *Servant Leadership: A Journey into the Nature of Legitimate Power & Greatness* (Mahway, NJ: Paulist Press, 1977).

[RHEM2020] Reed Hastings and Erin Meyer, *No Rules Rules: Netflix and the Culture of Reinvention* (New York: Penguin, 2020).

[RRTM2020] Ryan Ripley and Todd Miller, *Fixing Your Scrum: Practical Solutions to Common Scrum Problems* (Raleigh, NC: Pragmatic Bookshelf, 2020).

[RS2015] Richard Sheridan, *Joy, Inc.: How We Built a Workplace People Love* (Northwood, UK: Portfolio, 2015).

[RS2018] Richard Sheridan, *Chief Joy Officer: How Great Leaders Elevate Human Energy and Eliminate Fear* (Northwood, UK: Portfolio, 2018).

[SL2022] Sylvain Landry, *Bringing Scientific Thinking to Life: An Introduction to Toyota Kata for Next-Generation Business Leaders* (Montreal: JFD, 2022).

[SP2005] Stanley Pollack, *Moving Beyond Icebreakers: An Innovative Approach to Group Facilitation, Learning, and Action* (Boston: Center for Teen Empowerment, 2005).

[SS2010] Steven J. Spear, *The High-Velocity Edge: How Market Leaders Leverage Operational Excellence to Beat the Competition*, Second Edition (New York: McGraw Hill, 2010).

[TF2022] Traci Fenton, *Freedom at Work: The Leadership Strategy for Transforming Your Life, Your Organization, and Our World* (Dallas, TX: BenBella Books, 2022).

[TK2009] Tom Kelley, *The Art of Innovation: Lessons in Creativity for IDEP, America's Leading Design Firm* (New York: Currency, 2001).

[TO1988] Taiichi Ohno, *Toyota Production System: Beyond Large-Scale Production* (New York: Productivity Press, 1988).

[US1983] United States, National Commission on Excellence in Education, "A Nation at Risk: The Imperative for Educational Reform" (1983).

Index

X–Y–Z

Register Your Product at informit.com/register

Access additional benefits and save up to 65%* on your next purchase

- Automatically receive a coupon for 35% off books, eBooks, and web editions and 65% off video courses, valid for 30 days. Look for your code in your InformIT cart or the Manage Codes section of your account page.

- Download available product updates.

- Access bonus material if available.**

- Check the box to hear from us and receive exclusive offers on new editions and related products.

InformIT—The Trusted Technology Learning Source

InformIT is the online home of information technology brands at Pearson, the world's leading learning company. At informit.com, you can

- Shop our books, eBooks, and video training. Most eBooks are DRM-Free and include PDF and EPUB files.

- Take advantage of our special offers and promotions (informit.com/promotions).

- Sign up for special offers and content newsletter (informit.com/newsletters).

- Access thousands of free chapters and video lessons.

- Enjoy free ground shipping on U.S. orders.*

* Offers subject to change.

** Registration benefits vary by product. Benefits will be listed on your account page under Registered Products.

Connect with InformIT—Visit informit.com/community

 Pearson

Addison-Wesley • Adobe Press • Cisco Press • Microsoft Press • Oracle Press • Peachpit Press • Pearson IT Certification • Que